FROM BUSSING ~ TO BUGGING

The BEST in congressional HUMOR

"FROM BUSSING TO BUGGING"

The BEST in congressional HUMOR

ANGELE de T. GINGRAS

 PUBLISHED BY **ACROPOLIS BOOKS LTD.** • WASHINGTON, D.C. 20009

ACROPOLIS BOOKS LTD.
*Colortone Building, 2400 17th St., N.W.
Washington, D.C. 20009*

Printed in the United States of America by
Colortone Creative Graphics Inc., *Washington, D.C. 20009*

*Type set in Mallard
by Colortone Typographic Division, Inc.*

Design by Design and Art Studio 2400, Inc.

Library of Congress Catalog Number 72-12394

International Standard Book No. 87491-344-6 (cloth)
87491-345-4 (paper)

Laughword

The laughs surfacing on Capitol Hill, where the elected representatives of the people go about their business of lawmaking, help to keep the democratic ship of state on an even keel, and to steer it safely through some troubled and muddied waters.

Here and there, stirred into the serious business of legislating, members of Congress indulge in irony, satire, anecdotes, antiquated bromides, and verbal horseplay. Some of it is original. Some of it is drafted by a ghost writer, or pinched from Flip Wilson and adjusted to the congressman's oratorical and laugh style. It is dished in speeches on the floor of the Senate and House of Representatives, at hearings of congressional committees, in talks at press clubs, conventions, conferences, graduation ceremonies, political rallies, banquets, and in exchanges on the Washington party circuit and in the Democratic and Republican cloakrooms . . . wherever some choice words will say what the member of Congress wants to say about legislation or public affairs, or about why he should be elected or re-elected.

And when the Congress laughs, it is the nation laughing. The sound is much the same. Through these men and women who come from all parts of the country to the capital, the laughter reflects a basically cheerful, optimistic nation getting itself into perspective by laughing at itself, its mistakes, its vagaries, its humanity, its absurdities.

The many laugh variations indulged in by members of Congress are for the most part in the historical mainstream of American humor. In every Congress there are space age versions of crackerbox philosophers, and types who indulge in traditional rambling, leisurely, unstudied, good natured ribbing—the kind of talk that was heard in other times around the stove in the general store, and on the courthouse square. Sometimes there are men who dish earthy humor, like Democratic Representative Thomas Rees of California describing "The Day The Candidate Belched," or Democratic Representative Gillespie (Sonny) V. Montgomery announcing on the floor of the House of Representatives a tobacco spitting contest down in Mississippi. There are tall story tellers in the mood of Paul Bunyan and Mike Fink, dispensers of frontier humor in the Davy Crockett groove, and congressmen turning into slaphappy, over-zealous Yankee peddlers and medicine show men, to describe the products of their states, and to put over reasons why they should be elected or re-elected. Black humor has also surfaced on Capitol Hill in the wake of the Watergate scandal and other political fiascos. In this increasingly popular putdown laughter, in this era of the putdown, no holds are barred in subject and modes of attack. The mood is that of Kafka and Beckett and Marshall McLuhan. It says foolishness, not reason, often runs the world.

But only around the fringes of congressional wit and wisdom does an occasional obscenity or tasteless vulgarity intrude on the American humor mainstream, and it is rare and not a public utterance. Ask any member of Congress and he'll say why . . . no votes in it.

And if the reader doesn't find the congressional humor and wit in this volume as good as that of Will Rogers, Mark Twain, or Flip Wilson, he may at the next election, and within the democratic process, upgrade the laugh quotient for any revision of the book—he may put his ballot in the box for a funnier congressman.

In a Foreword, authors and editors of a book thank librarians, sources, indexers, friends who have read the manuscript without a fee and typists who have typed the manuscript accurately even with a plethora of insertions and interlinings. In a Laughword, authors or editors thank people who have contributed in one way or another to the survival of their laugh life—relatives and editors who have bought their humor when nobody else would, friends and colleagues with whom they have exchanged funny stories . . . especially those whose laughter has been removed by the inevitabilities of time and distance. In the Laughword of this book of political humor, I wish to thank all of these people but particularly my father, Georges Joseph Gingras; my mother, Anna d'Iriarte de Tranaltes Gingras; my sisters Helene and Lucie; my brother Georges; my writing grandfather, Fernand d'Iriarte de Tranaltes; the Watneys of France and England; Nicholas Cantacuzene of old St. Petersburg and Switzerland; Admiral Virgilio Ribeiro of Portugal; Dr. and Mrs. John Crane-Cirne of Arizona and Brazil, and their father, Maj. Gen. H. K. Rutherford; the Symonds of England and the United States; the Mowrers and Adams; and my literary agent, Mrs. Maxwell Aley.

Contents

Chapters

CHAPTER ONE

A California Congressman Ruffs Up Nixon's Palace Guard

GILBERT AND SULLIVAN ALIVE AND WELL

Sometimes the target for political irony by a member of Congress is a many splendored thing, as when Richard Nixon tried to dress up the White House police force in the sartorial mood of ancient Balkan kingdoms.

A congressman of the President's own party and home state, Representative Charles H. Wilson of California, ripped up this side order of ruffles and flourishes on the floor of the House of Representatives.

Mr. Speaker, although the doctors consistently warn against it, I am afraid I had no choice the other night as I watched the late news but to let my heart swell with grand and glorious pride as I watched the opulence, the splendor, the pageantry, and the pride of my country's highest officer surrounded grandiloquently by a bevy of palace guards decked out in such resplendence and majesty as to move the hearts and minds of the most exalted and revered emperors in all the world's history.

Mr. Speaker, let me assure you and my distinguished colleagues that Gilbert and Sullivan are alive and well, tucked neatly away within the confines of the White House or, as it soon may be called, the Alabaster Palace.

The Pirates of Penzance had nothing on the newly refurbished White House police guard uniforms. In their softly shaded buttermilk tunics, topped with ebony vinyl caps fit for a Kaiser's fondest dreams, they are worthy to line the Grand Canal for the passage of a royal barge—perhaps even the H.M.S. Pinafore.

REPUBLICAN REPRESENTATIVE CHARLES WILSON: The White House police guard in their softly shaded buttermilk tunics, topped with ebony vinyl caps fit for a Kaiser's fondest dreams . . .

Certainly we are all familiar with the stories of President George Washington's difficult decision about how he, as the leader of a newly independent land settled largely by refugees from imperial Europe and the British monarchy, should be addressed. What title would be proper? Most exalted ruler? Too gushy. King? That reeked of rulers past. President? President was perfect—thoroughly adequate, carrying all the dignity necessary for the new leader without alluding to any of the less savory characteristics of nations fled. Having now seen President Nixon's latter-day palace guard, I feel I must ask, will George Washington's humble decision stand? Or will San Clemente cease to be affectionately known as the "Western White House" and soon be dubbed the "Summer Palace"? Might the President contemplate trading his bombproof Lincoln for a coach and four? Who can say?

One thing is clear. President Nixon apparently brought back more than foreign policy ideas from his trips around the globe last year. While Charles de Gaulle may have now faded from earlier prominence, the historical rulers of imperial Europe are obviously on the comeback trail. Judging from Tuesday's reception on the White House lawn for British Prime Minister Harold Wilson, Mr. Nixon evidently has some very definite ideas about what "splendor in the grass" can mean to a foreign dignitary.

A Side Order of Ruffles and Flourishes

If we are to believe the pundits who claim that Prime Minister Wilson can use the favorable publicity of an impressive Washington welcome in his next election campaign, and if we are to believe the historians who tell us that the British people have always had a soft spot for pomp and circumstance, it appears as though Mr. Wilson could be headed for a cream-colored, vinyl-topped landslide with a generous side order of ruffles and flourishes.

It is most difficult to refrain from imagining what manner of pomp the President may be reserving for future visitors to the shrine of 1600 Pennsylvania Avenue, N.W. Perhaps the circle drive, paved with Aztec gold for the leader of our Mexican neighbors to the south. Maybe richly woven oriental rugs stretching across the less resplendent crabgrass for our Asian friends. And why not an orange roof for weary travelers and Astroturf for the Nation's Number One football team—if such a distinction will ever be ventured again. Surely the horizons of hospitality are broad and limitless.

It is said that we have passed into the era of a pastel, cloth coat administration. Our mistake, of course, was to fail to realize that this was to be a universally applied characteristic. The Nixon Doctrine may not be all things to all men, but it is certainly some things to some men—including the White House police.

In all seriousness, let me state that I do not for a moment question the President's right to add a few personal touches to his surroundings. He is not the first President to do so and he is unlikely to be the last. And the White House is certainly the place for class and dignity. Let me be very clear about that.

Simple Fare as Baloney Sandwiches

At $95 apiece these one hundred uniforms are perhaps less inflationary than such outrageous items as hospital construction, library books, and cancer research. If the President feels more secure requesting more antiballistic missiles and vetoing Health, Education, and Welfare measures from an oval throneroom, safely protected by an elite corps of elegantly attired guardsmen, this is clearly his privilege. And if the policemen feel a bit strange eating such simple fare as baloney sandwiches while dressed to the teeth, then let them eat cake. After all, he is the President. Make no mistake about that.

The fancy uniforms were never again seen on the White House police force.

SENATOR
JOHN F. KENNEDY

CHAPTER TWO

Senator Hugh Scott Writes to JFK

BACK AT LYNDON'S OTHER RANCH

Almost any election year Senator Hugh Scott of Pennsylvania has something to say about other legislators off in far away places campaigning for the Presidency. During 1972, Democratic Senator George McGovern of South Dakota was a favorite target. But it was some years before, when Senator John F. Kennedy was busily trying for the Democratic presidential nomination, that the Republican Minority Leader reached an ironical crescendo in this area.

One Thursday, the then Senator from Massachusetts attended commencement ceremonies at Harvard University and later in the day went on the "Jack Paar Show." Senator Scott addressed him on the subject:

Dear Jack:

Thursday was a big day down here, back at Lyndon's other ranch. I thought you would like a fill-in on some important developments you might have missed while you were absent from the Senate on Thursday.

The Long Arm of Your Leadership

I am sure you will appreciate this note because it indicates that we in the Senate took very seriously the lecture you had delivered to us only two days before on the importance of leadership and the need to do something about the missile programs and about modernizing the armed forces.

SENATOR HUGH SCOTT (right) TO JFK: Thursday was a big day down here, back at Lyndon's other ranch. Official Senate Photo

You will be glad to know that the long arm of your leadership reaching all the way from Cambridge, Massachusetts, was felt on the Senate floor and we responded faithfully. The Senate passed the $40.5 billion Defense Appropriations Bill and we put in a 25,000 man increase in the Marine Corps.

You will also be glad to know, Jack, that we added $90 million more for modernization of the Army. We are going to wait until you return before we tackle the foreign aid bill because your colleagues over on the House side have knocked off 3/4 billion dollars from that bill and we know how you feel about it.

So, when you get back, please exert the leadership you called for in your "State of the Union Message" and see that we put that money back so that our foreign aid program won't be seriously impaired.

That wasn't the only thing we did yesterday, Jack. It was a real busy day. We passed a Constitutional Amendment to permit citizens of the District of Columbia to vote for President and Vice President and to have three votes in the Electoral College. We know how much you wanted this, Jack, because we have heard you advocate home rule, for you would want us to support this Constitutional Amendment.

It was such a busy day, Jack, that we also took care of the housing bill for you, as we know that you as a presidential candidate have strongly advocated more and better housing. So, we passed a one-and-a-quarter-billion-dollar housing bill, and we hope you like it, because we tried to put in everything we felt you would want.

Top Hat and Tails of an Overseer

There were a number of speeches made on these bills and there were a couple of close votes on the housing bill. But we knew you were busy and we did the best we could.

We know that you must have enjoyed your college reunion back at Harvard because we read all about your being there and how you were dressed in the traditional top hat and tails of an overseer. That was nice.

The message in your "State of the Union" speech last Tuesday inspired us and we want you to know that we hope that you have enjoyed the state of the reunion at college. I imagine you must have seen the usual parade and the cavorting of the eternal sophomores and the usual excitement which goes with commencement. What fun it must have been!

Well, it was a long day, Jack. After being in session fourteen hours, we trod our weary way homeward. A number of Senators had made sacrifices to stay here in the Senate. Some had canceled speeches before large groups of people, some had postponed the mending of their political fences at home, and at least one Senator had declined an honorary degree in order to be able to vote on these big tax-heavy bills.

We know that you have called for sacrifices by everybody in your speeches around the country and we want you to know, Jack, that we were very glad to make these sacrifices in the interest of the national defense and the welfare of our citizens and the civil rights of the residents of the District of Columbia. You would have been proud of us, Jack.

We Could Use Some Less Toil, Too

It was real refreshing to come home dog tired after those weary fourteen hours of Senate debate and turn on the TV to our favorite "lipstick and gin-mix" show, presided over by one of your most enthusiastic admirers. You and the other Jack were also selling something called "lestoil." I want you to know that we had more toil than we wanted yesterday and we could use some less toil, too.

With what joy we observed your appearance on this show and your sparkling answers to the happy, responsive audience. We were glad that you looked so relaxed and so "unwearied of toil." This is one of the advantages of youth, Jack, and never, never forget it.

Since I did not see you around on Friday, either, perhaps I'll get a chance later to report to you about the debate on the federal and postal employees pay raise bill.

Well, we don't want to bore you, Jack. If you have time, drop in and if not, just send one of the other Kennedys down.

EYED EACH OTHER SUSPICIOUSLY

And at the Al Smith Memorial Dinner in New York, the absent John F. Kennedy, then a senator, was prefacing his own remarks with laughs:

I am glad to be here at this notable dinner once again, and I am glad that Mr. Nixon is here also. Now that Cardinal Spellman has demonstrated the proper spirit, I assume that shortly I will be invited to a Quaker dinner honoring Herbert Hoover.

Cardinal Spellman is the only man so widely respected in American politics that he could bring together, amicably at the same banquet table, for the first time in this campaign, two political leaders who are increasingly apprehensive about the November election—who have long eyed each other suspiciously, and who have disagreed so strongly, both publicly and privately, Vice President Nixon and Governor Rockefeller.

Mr. Nixon, like the rest of us, has had his troubles in this campaign. At one point even the Wall Street Journal was criticizing his tactics. This is like the Observatore Romano criticizing the Pope.

But I think the worst news for the Republicans this week was that Casey Stengel has been fired. It must show that perhaps experience does not count.

On this matter of experience, I had announced earlier this year that if successful I would not consider campaign contributions as a substitute for experience in appointing ambassadors. Ever since I made that statement I have not received one single cent from my father.

One of the inspiring notes that was struck in the last debate was struck by the Vice President in his moving warning to the children of the nation and the candidates against the use of profanity by Presidents and ex-Presidents when they are on the stump. And I know after fourteen years in the Congress with the Vice President that he was very sincere in his views about the use of profanity. But I am told that a prominent Republican said to him yesterday in Jacksonville, Florida, "Mr. President, that was a damn fine speech." And the Vice President said, "I appreciate the compliment but not the language." And the Republican went on, "Yes, sir, I liked it so much that I contributed a thousand dollars to your campaign." And Mr. Nixon replied, "The hell you say."

However, I would not want to give the impression that I am taking former President Truman's use of language lightly. I have sent him the following wire: "Dear Mr. President: I have noted with interest your suggestion as to where those who vote for my opponent should go. While I understand and symphathize with your deep motivation, I think it is important that our side try to refrain from raising the religious issue. . . ."

*   *   *

And his brother, the future Attorney General and Senator, Robert F. Kennedy, was saying at political rallies: "My brother Jack couldn't be here. My mother couldn't be here. My sister Eunice couldn't be here, my sister Pat couldn't be here, my sister Jean couldn't be here, but if my brother Jack were here he'd tell you Lodge has a very bad voting record."

HENRY KISSINGER: Can't make it tonight. I'm posing for the centerfold of the Kiplinger Letter.   Dev O'Neill Photo

CHAPTER THREE

Campaign Rhetoric of the Also-rans

KISSINGER IN KIPLINGER CENTERFOLD

Any election year the losing candidates for the presidential election are also the source and the target for everything from blistering or corny one-liners to extended rhetoric. 1972 was no exception.

In the spring Arizona's Senator Barry Goldwater told his Gridiron Club audience in Washington, Henry Kissinger couldn't be at the dinner. President Nixon's foreign policy adviser was busy posing for the centerfold of the Kiplinger Letter. And the 1964 Republican presidential candidate noted Senator John Tunney wouldn't attend either. The California Democrat was taking elocution lessons in Hyannisport. He then pointed out that when Spiro Agnew speaks, he gets action. The Vice President made one talk calling for a lower profile, and two million young women quit wearing brassieres.

Senator Hubert Humphrey told guests at the same dinner he understood the Republican Vice President was in Palm Springs with Frank Sinatra, and Frank was giving him retirement lessons. Also that Senator Bill Proxmire wouldn't be eating with them. The Wisconsin Democrat was getting hair transplants . . . having his hair put in while the rest of the country was pulling theirs out. And at another dinner given by the Washington Press Club, Democratic Senator Frank Church of Idaho was saying the Vice President was eating fortune cookies—ten pounds a day—looking for the one that would tell him he'd be on the ticket again, and Bebe Rebozo was studying Chinese real estate, figuring out ways to subdivide China.

SENATOR WILLIAM PROXMIRE OF WISCONSIN: Who said that about me having hair transplants while everybody else was pulling theirs out?
Dev O'Neill Photo

GEE HOW THEY RUN

In March, House Minority Leader Gerald Ford of Michigan was asking a New Hampshire political rally if they heard about the Democratic presidential candidate who was so worried about air pollution, he cancelled six speeches. Senator Hugh Scott complained when the networks decided to give the Democrats almost twice the half hour of air time allotted Nixon for his address to the Congress. Then he added, "All I can observe is that they probably need it." After Governor George Wallace of Alabama won his stunning victory in the Florida Democratic presidential primary in the spring of 1972, Scott said, "The outstretched palms of Florida have been crossed and many of the candidates have been double-crossed." And Republican William B. Saxbe of Ohio was saying some candidate or other was still back in the nuts and berries stage.

A little later that year, Vice President Agnew, nominally the President of the Senate, was telling Nassau County, New York, Republicans, Senator Edmund Muskie of Maine was the ultimate in political shuttle-cocks. The candidate for the Democratic presidential nomination had tossed his stovepipe lid into the ring so often it was beginning to look like a sat-on collapsible opera hat. On Lincoln's birthday Wyoming's Republican Senator Clifford P. Hansen was saying a Democratic party official was looking for a bright dynamic candidate who could electrify the voters and lead the party into the White House. When Senator Muskie said, "Here I am," the official replied, "Good. You can help me look!" When Senator Hubert H. Humphrey of Minnesota began moving ahead of Muskie in the Gallup Poll during the 1972 race, Scott proposed that the Democrats again choose a Humphrey-Muskie ticket. "I see no reason for breaking up a losing team," he added.

HAZY AS A STONED HIPPIE

Vice President Agnew was also saying Senator George McGovern's stand on marijuana was as hazy as that of a stoned hippie. On crime, Agnew said the Democrat from South Dakota vacillated like an over-wound metronome.

And the campaign had hardly begun swinging when Democratic presidential nominee McGovern himself was saying President Nixon's taking credit for increased Social Security benefits was like Scrooge trying to take credit for Christmas. And Senator Edmund Muskie, when he returned to Washington after his withdrawal from the race for the Democratic presidential nomination, was telling the National Press Club

SENATOR GEORGE McGOVERN OF SOUTH DAKOTA: President Nixon taking credit for increased Social Security benefits is like Scrooge trying to take credit for Christmas.

Dev O'Neill Photo

he would run for Vice President if he had the opportunity to start his campaign all over again, and have the primary system reformed in a way to permit him to win.

THE DAY THE CANDIDATE BELCHED

In several of his speeches, former Representative Emanuel Celler, Democrat of New York, once said the ideal congressman had the wisdom of a Solomon, perspicacity of a bill collector, curiosity of a cat, cunning of a fox, thick skin of an elephant, eagerness of a beaver, amiability of a lapdog, kindness of a loving wife, diplomacy of a wayward husband, and the good humor of an idiot.

In the election year 1972, this longer comment, "The Day the Candidate Belched" by Democratic Representative Thomas Rees of California, suggests a digestive system lined with steel would also be the greatest for any politician running for office, but particularly for a presidential candidate. And at the same time if the verb "wept" were substituted for "belched," the California Democrat wrapped up in a very perceptive wordshell the purported effect on his nomination of Senator Muskie's crying in the snow in front of a New Hampshire newspaper one very cold day.

*   *   *

It had been an exhausting day. The presidential candidate had risen at 4:30 a.m. to catch a plane. When he arrived at the city his schedule began with a briefing and then a cold scrambled egg breakfast with the local Chamber of Commerce; brunch with the shop stewards at the plant; a pizza lunch with the Sons of Italy; Polish sausage at the Kosciusko High School; and then a cocktail reception at the B'nai B'rith with, of course, the obligatory lox. That left ten minutes to get ready for the fund-raising banquet.

All this time there were crowds pressing in with outstretched hands. Along with them came the newsmen—shoving their microphones at the candidate's mouth every time it opened—and the television men with their lights and zoom lenses, tripping over their soundmen. All the while the candidate was full of sweetness and light even though the pizza had been cold, the sausage greasy, and the drink tepid.

The banquet proved to be more of the same. The room was overheated, the orchestra oppressively loud and corny, and the well-wishers incessant. The meal was a disaster—soggy breaded veal cutlet fried in a deep batter to hide the gristle, discolored shrunken peas, and canned fruit salad for dessert.

It was now time for the candidate to speak after having listened to countless invocations long enough to detail the entire party platform, pronounced by aging members of the party's hierarchy. As he rose, looking out over the audience, feeling the weariness of a fourteen-hour day, and glancing at the clustered battery of television cameras, radio mikes, and newsmen, this man—who might well become the President of the United States—belched!

That did it. The audience was stunned. The belch was recorded by four networks, and fifteen local stations, and BBC. The national commentators and the opposition had a full day. The candidate, who had the reputation of being a man of dignity, strength of character, and good manners, became a slob overnight.

Despite numerous medical statements corroborating the fact that pizza, Polish sausage, greasy breaded cutlet, and canned fruit salad could cause an individual to belch, the public was shocked and dismayed. The people might belch—but a presidential candidate, NEVER, especially not in public. What would happen, the theorists projected, if the candidate was elected President and belched at a summit meeting? "But in some cultures belching is apropos," countered the campaign egghead. "Look at China, for instance. If you don't belch there after eating, the host will think you don't like the meal!"

But no, argued the national press media, in that case a president belches because he has a duty to do so; that's different from belching when you're not supposed to belch.

If the belchers of America had unified behind the candidate, he would have won by a landslide. But instead the belchers were embarrassed and indignant—presidential candidates were not supposed to be like them. . . .

The presidential candidate lost.

VOTED FOR NIXON AND GOT HUMPHREY

Early in 1972, Democratic Representative Robert H. Mollohan of West Virginia told the Jaycees of Marietta, Ohio:

. . . Now the anti-war Liberals used to complain that in 1964 they voted for Johnson and got Goldwater anyway. Today some of the conservatives are complaining that they voted for Nixon in 1968 and got Humphrey anyway.

But it could be worse. Can you imagine what Barry Goldwater would have said if President Humphrey had visited Red China? Can you imagine what Governor Reagan would have said if President Humphrey had proposed an expanded trade with Russia?

But we shouldn't complain about the Democrats having so many candidates. Think of all the money they are going to bring into my state for the West Virginia primary.

Abandoned Coal Mines and Ghost Towns

Now if we could just get Teddy Kennedy into the campaign, the state could enjoy the benefit of the Kennedy millions during the primary campaign and the Rockefeller millions during the general election.

And of course when the Democrats come to West Virginia to campaign, they have to look for poverty and abuses against the environment, and in general bemoan the present situation and call for new leadership.

And we are in Governor Moore's debt for realizing this and offering to provide a selection of abandoned coal mines and ghost towns for the purpose for just a small fee.

But election campaigns can also create a debate on many issues. In welfare reform, the Congress and the Administration haven't been able to agree on who has qualified. The White House asked for welfare for Penn Central, Lockheed, and the SST, but the Congress decided that the SST should get out and look for a job, and Penn Central went bankrupt anyway. Lockheed, however, did qualify for welfare and is doing nicely now. And if any of you have been watching NBC News this week, you will have realized that the milk producers also received an increase in their allowance, but not until they paid their respects at the White House. The best estimate of what it cost to pay those respects was about $350,000 for the President's campaign war chest. . . .

*   *   *

At the same time Republican Senator Robert Dole of Kansas, who was until recently Chairman of the Republican National Committee, was calling Senator McGovern a fellow who would try to twist the arm of the Almighty to gain public office, and suggested he be given television time to debate himself. And when it was all over and Nixon had won a landslide victory, Dole summed it up by saying the Republicans got the top prize, but lost a lot of door prizes; and the role of Senator McGovern in the Senate would be a new one: he would be there.

MORE LIKE A FROST HEAVE

And because a lot of people like to remember another very special election year—1968—on the eve of the New Hampshire primary, Senator McCarthy was asked if he felt a groundswell. "It feels more like a frost heave," he answered.

When President Johnson withdrew from the presidential race before the Wisconsin primary, McCarthy said, "After what I thought was a rather serious race between me and the President, we made the last turn for home and he jumped over the fence and started to eat the grass on the infield. I was a little bit embarrassed to go on down the home stretch to the wire under those circumstances."

And the magazine *New Republic* reports that when Senator McCarthy was asked what his supporters would do if it came to a choice between Nixon and Johnson, he answered, "That's like choosing between vulgarity and obscenity, isn't it?"

When Arthur Schlesinger, Jr., departed from his staff, McCarthy said, "Losing Arthur has about as much impact as being dented by a leaf."

And in the spring of 1968, Representative Gerald R. Ford, Minority Leader of the House of Representatives, was saying at the Gridiron Club in Washington:

. . . I've heard that President Johnson tells his visitors: "There's nothing wrong with Jerry Ford except he played football too long . . . without a helmet.". . . Why did I ever tell Nat Finney I wanted to be the next Republican Speaker? Matching me against Hubert Humphrey for laughs is like putting Twiggy against Zsa Zsa Gabor. . . .

CHAPTER FOUR

Poormouthing in Rags-to-Riches Groove

CORNBREAD AND MOLASSES IN LUNCH BAG

In the Congress traditional patterns of American thinking sometimes create a rare twist in the nation's humor.

Anecdotes in the poormouthing, rags-to-riches, Horatio Alger groove, for example, are forever appearing in speeches of members of the Senate and House, and some of them are inversions of the bragging, boasting frontier tall story.

Representative Kenneth Gray says he was born in the Hoover Depression, when things were so slow, the Mississippi and Ohio Rivers were running only two days a week. The Illinois Democrat's parents were so poor they couldn't have children, so the neighbors had him. He walked twelve miles to school, took cornbread and molasses in his lunch bag, and describes a winter when his father's truck got stuck in the mud, and stayed on the road all winter until the family could buy a gallon of gas to get it moving again.

A lot of this political poormouthing runs to early job talk.

Senator John O. Pastore admits proudly to having been a kicker in his early days. And it didn't have anything to do with football quarterbacking at a fashionable New England prep school. The Rhode Island Democrat said he paid his way through high school by operating a foot press in a jewelry factory in Providence. Tired feet inspired him to get on to clerking in the Narragansett Electric Company, so he could finish law school at night.

OHIO REPRESENTATIVE KEN GRAY: With meat prices what they are!
Dev O'Neill Photo

GALLAGHER WAS SECOND BROOM

Former Democratic Representative Cornelius Gallagher of New Jersey said he owed his whole congressional career to certain job insecurities of the Depression. When he was graduated from high school, he went to work as "Second Broom" or assistant sweeper at the Electro-Dynamic Company in Bayonne, New Jersey, at 55 cents an hour. He said if he had had the security of being "First Broom" he never would have gone to college and law school at night. As it was, he was afraid the company would decide they only needed a "First Broom," would abolish the "Second Broom," and he wouldn't have a job.

The life of former Democratic Representative Harlan Hagan of California might also have been different if he had been the first can stacker instead of the second can stacker at a Del Monte plant. At one point in the job routine, Hagan threw a tray with ten cans to the second stacker who was then on top of six-foot piles of cans. Paid by the piece, Hagan's eye on the main chance sometimes made him miss. If he'd been in the safe top berth of the first stacker, he might never have moved on to the less hazardous job of washing dishes in a woman's boarding house.

CUSTOMERS BOILING IN OIL

And, of course, in their speeches the Texans always have something colorful and rugged to add to the annals of congressional poverty dropping.

At least a couple of congressmen from the Lone Star State worked their way through college by removing termites from under houses and have some interesting sidelights to offer in their speeches on the subject.

Democratic Representative Henry B. Gonzalez says he didn't last long under the house. The smell of oil quickly removed him to higher and more hazardous levels. It seems the owner of the termite exterminating company used kerosene oil exclusively in its war on the bug. Customers began to say the oil odor after the debugging was worse than what it cured! Young Gonzalez, who had a talent for the spoken word and for public relating, was taken from under the house by the head exterminator, and sent out to soothe the customers who were boiling in oil.

On this above the house level Gonzalez learned to dodge flying objects and temper derogatory language, but says he soon moved to the haven of a Chinese grocery store, where he picked up a few friends and a mastery of Chinese cuss words.

Democratic Representative Bob Casey, also an exterminator while he attended the University of Houston at night, said the experience taught him how to recognize a termite, and that he better continue in school if he ever wanted to get out from under the house.

*   *   *

And there have been some members of Congress excluded by the nature of things from the Hill's poormouthing in speeches. A congressman who has been caught in some unfortunate poverty pockets in his own childhood, explained in one of his speeches why a rich man doesn't belong. The comments of the congressman who prefers to have his feet remain anonymous were triggered by the late millionaire Senator Robert F. Kennedy's launching of a drive at the New York World's Fair for used shoes for poverty-stricken Appalachian children. He did this by donating a box full of footwear from his then nine children. During his speech protesting the millionaire Kennedy's donation, the congressman took off one of his own shoes, and displayed his really rough bunions.

"Those are on my feet because I wore used shoes. Let's get it over to this Kennedy fellow that the children of Appalachia would better be kept in a healthy natural barefoot state, unless we can give them shoes that are fitted to their individual feet," he said.

The Congressman suggested the then two millionaire Senators Kennedy from New York and Massachusetts might be better advised to get on this poverty dropping bandwagon in another way. They could talk up their Kennedy and Honey Fitz grandfathers, who came from Ireland with little more than a feather bed.

Democratic Senator Quentin Burdick of North Dakota, however, also poverty drops but not from his own cup of potliquor. His father was a member of Congress, and in a financial position to get his children through colleges, even in the Depression years. But that didn't keep Quentin out of the poor club. When he was graduated from the University of Minnesota Law School, the dirt-poor, drought-poor North Dakota farmers flocked to him for help in their fight with the banks for crop loans.

By the time young Quentin had gotten those farmers through the next ten years and into the plusher 1940's, he had vicariously experienced a lot of poverty. It gave him enough Tobacco Road and Appalachia brand of poormouthing to last him for a long lifetime of speeches.

BAREFOOT SANDERS OF TURTLE CREEK DRIVE

Sometimes, of course, some man aspiring to the national legislature goes the whole hog on this kind of thing, and loses the political ball game.

An assistant attorney general in the Johnson Administration who ran for the Senate Democratic primaries race in Texas in 1972, was called Barefoot Sanders, and he lived on Turtle Creek Drive in Dallas. He had overwritten himself by the accidents of a name and an address. He lost.

And, of course, poormouthing or poverty dropping in speeches snowballed during the Johnson-Humphrey Administration, when there was much talk about poverty pockets, ghettoes, and Appalachia, and the Great Society, Head Start, and the Poverty and Job Corps, which would do something about these things.

The late President Lyndon Johnson, when he was in the Senate and in the White House, was forever talking about the garage he lived in when he was in college. No edifice could have had all the drafts, beer cans, bugs, rodents, offensive odors, and other nasties Johnson put into it. The health authorities of the State of Texas and the nation would have picketed the place. And Senator Hubert Humphrey was forever telling how Mrs. Humphrey sold sandwiches to put him through graduate school. To listen to Hubert, Muriel handled enough tunafish, ham salad, and onion cheese spread in the hours before the dawn of every day to feed the student body of three universities.

Former Democratic Representative Andy Jacobs of Indiana goes all the poormouthers one better with some vicarious poormouthing. He tells about a local Indiana politician who said he wasn't born in a log cabin, but his family moved into one as soon as they could afford it.

DEMOCRATIC REPRESENTATIVE JAMES SYMINGTON OF MISSOURI: If Grandfather had been born here, I would be President today.

SENATOR HERMAN TALMADGE: With single such vehicle, we could transport the distinguished Supreme Court members each morning to their place of employme

CHAPTER FIVE

Supreme Court in a Yellow Bus

WHO'S THAT IN THE LITTLE OLE BUS?

Sometimes a member of Congress doesn't dig a decision of the Supreme Court, and uses the politics of humor to show his position on the subject.

The bussing of children to public schools to achieve integration, which stems from a high court ruling, inspires Capitol Hill to everything from satire to political burlesque. An ironical contribution in this area was made by Democratic Senator Herman Talmadge of Georgia. He got in his political lick on the floor of the Senate in June of 1972, when other legislation on appropriating funds to furnish justices of the Supreme Court a limousine and chauffeur, was being considered.

Mr. President, I would like to direct the attention of the Senate to a serious transportation crisis which exists in our nation's capital. I refer to the problems which the members of the Supreme Court are encountering in getting to and from work every day. This problem has recently grown acute due to the flight of the justices to the suburbs so that they can be closer to the private schools which their children and grandchildren populate in great numbers. The Administration moved to meet this emergency by suggesting that each member of the Court be given his own driver and limousine. The Committee has compromised by providing funds in the amount of $14,000 for a car and driver for the Chief Justice.

Yellow School Bus to Transport the Justices

It occurs to me that perhaps we could arrive at a solution which would adequately and appropriately meet this problem and alleviate trouble spots which exist in several other areas as well.

My staff has instituted extensive inquiries among experts in the transportation industry. I am told that for no more than $1,000 an extremely utilitarian and attractive, though slightly used, vehicle could be secured which would admirably meet this crisis. This all-purpose vehicle has traditionally been used to transport students to and from school, primarily in the southern states. But it is easily adaptable for other uses. I refer, of course, to that reliable mechanical beast of burden which is second only to the little red school house as an American institution—the yellow school bus.

It is a matter of record that the justices themselves are ardent supporters of this method of transportation. In the great American tradition of selfless patriotism, however, they have not tried to selfishly secure for themselves the benefits which they have so freely distributed to others. With a single such vehicle, we could transport these distinguished jurists in a body, each morning, to their place of employment.

By this one simple stroke, we could do even more than relieve the transportation crisis. As the result of actions taken last year by the Appropriations Committee, unemployment runs rampant in the ranks of chauffeurs and drivers in the District of Columbia. In the District of Columbia government alone no less than forty-eight of these drivers were cut from the employment rolls last year. We could reduce this figure by almost 5 percent by employing a driver and guard for the bus.

Striking a Blow for Clean Air

But the benefits do not stop here. One school bus would cause insignificantly less air and noise pollution than would the nine limousines. We would be striking a blow for clean air.

In all fairness, however, all would not be roses as the result of my proposal. There would also be some thorns, I am sad to say. The justices would have to get up before day, stand in the sleet and the snow, to return home after dark. No longer would the suburban neighborhoods ring with the glad shouts of the justices at play in the afternoon after Court was out. But they are not without recourse. Should this new form of transportation endanger their health or significantly impinge upon their educational processes, we could implore the President to step in and *declare a moratorium on this busing. Of course, this step could only be taken after due deliberation and the taking of several polls among the electorate.*

I want to point out to the Senate that we are moving with caution in this area. If this revolutionary transportation scheme should prove effective, it could be expanded to the ranks of the district and appellate court judges. Who knows, Mr. President, we might even expand the concept developed in this pilot study to include the ranks of neglected HEW bureaucrats who are slowed in their self-appointed mission to save our children by the traffic jams they must contend with every morning.

IN A HUDDLE ON THEIR KNEES

When another controversial topic involving the Supreme Court—reciting prayers in the public schools—was being debated on the Senate floor in early 1967, Democratic Senator Sam Ervin of North Carolina had this to say on the subject:

It's very fortunate for the Bar of the United States that the Supreme Court cannot explain its own prior decisions with the clarity with which a North Carolina School teacher explained the recent school prayer cases. This teacher went into her classroom about fifteen minutes before the class was supposed to begin work and caught a bunch of her boys down in a huddle on their knees in the corner of the room. She demanded of them what they were doing, and one of them hollered back and said, "We are shooting craps." She said, "That's all right, I was afraid you were praying."

*　　*　　*

And sometimes a member of Congress is not above using a little pressure on the Supreme Court at its highest jurisdictional level. Senator Hugh Scott wrote this letter in early January to the Chief Justice of the Supreme Court, Warren Burger, when that distinguished gentleman made some verbal moves in the direction of banning smoking on those fast metroliners that whisk up to New York from Washington.

Dear Warren:

May I enter a mild disclaimer? Or should I back off with a mea culpa?

Mike Mansfield, Jerry Ford and I are pipe smokers. I am so far addicted that I would not, if I could help it, travel on Amtrak if solace be denied me.

Could, if it be dicta, obiter, some word go to the Secretary of DOT or to the King of the Rails, to the effect that pipe smokers may enjoy the use of some part of the presently interdicted area for the indulgence of their contemplative addiction?

May it please the court!

Cordially, Hugh Scott, Republican Leader.

HOGS ARE BEAUTIFUL!

CHAPTER SIX

Some of Their Best Friends Are Swine

HOG CAPITAL OF THE WORLD

Members of Congress like to boast about the products of their district and of their state. And when they do, they use in their politics of humor, all the ingenuity and variety traditional in the approach of the Yankee peddlers who traveled America's early roads.

Representatives from pork producing states sometimes try to out-boast each other about the porcine charms of their pigs.

On June 12, 1972, Republican Representative Paul Findley of Illinois had this to say on the floor of the House of Representatives:

Mr. Speaker, it is with great pride I call attention to a list of the nation's top four hundred hog counties, based on the 1969 farm census, that appears in the June issue of National Hog Farmer.

Pike County, Illinois, my home county, has advanced to the number two position, moving up from third place.

In 1969, Pike County farmers marketed 485,958 hogs and pigs. Pike County's population in the 1970 census was only 19,185. This means that over twenty-five are marketed for every man, woman, and child in the county.

I would also like to congratulate our colleague, Congressman Thomas Railsback of Illinois' 19th Congressional District. Henry County, located within his district, holds the number one position with a total of 554,834 hog sales in 1969.

Paraphrasing the immortal baseball pitcher, Satchel Page, I would like to warn Mr. Railsback and Henry County farmers. Do not look back: someone is gaining. The people of Pike County say, like the company that also found itself in second place: "We try harder."

Pittsfield, Illinois, Pike County seat and my hometown, truly deserves its title of "Hog Capital of the World."

And along with all pork lovers in the world, Pittsfield and Pike County residents proudly cheer—Hogs Are Beautiful.

*   *   *

A week later Republican Representative Tom Railsback of Illinois carried on:

Mr. Speaker, I take this opportunity to set the record straight. Congratulations to my good friend and distinguished colleague, Congressman Paul Findley, and Pike County, which he represents, for their number two position in the United States hog sales for 1969.

On the House floor last Monday, Representative Findley commended that well-deserving constituency and also commended Henry County—in my district—for its number one position in United States hog sales— 554,834 in 1969. He also added a challenge to the people of Henry County: "Do not look back; someone is gaining." Hogwash. Henry County has long been number one in hog sales, and the people of Henry County are not about to relinquish their title. I have worked with Congressman Findley on many matters of benefit to all Illinois residents, but on this one I must state that he has stars in his eyes.

Bravo, Henry County.

THE PICKED-ON PORKER

Three days later the hogs-are-beautiful dialogue was picked up by former Republican Representative Fred Schwengel of Iowa:

Mr. Speaker . . . my purpose here today, is to set the record straight with respect to the pork industry and the maligned pig. . . . These films (Keep America Beautiful) depict the hog as being stupid, and an animal of unclean habits. This is a serious error which I hope to correct here today. The National Pork Producers Council has spearheaded the drive to correct this image by their distribution of bright green and yellow buttons proclaiming, "Hogs Are Beautiful." My purpose here this afternoon is to further correct the record and the general image of that much maligned animal, the "picked on porker."

I like pigs, and I honestly believe that most pigs like me. Hogs are beautiful. Some of my best friends are hogs.

Like Patrick Henry, I care not what unfortunate remarks others may make, but as for me, I like pigs. Against all those who would besmirch them, I stand ready to speak in their defense—even on the floor of the House of Representatives of the United States Congress.

Don't Be a Pig in the Park

The pork industry in America is disturbed about the bad image that my countrymen are creating for this lowly farm animal. Last year the promotion agents for Keep America Beautiful came out with this slogan: DON'T BE A PIG IN THE PARK.

Long before this slogan was coined, there were other expressions in common use that the advertisers suspect have somehow cooled the market for pork products. And that is not hogwash—to use just one such expression.

To keep pace with the litterbug campaign, National Pork Producers Council has launched a counteroffensive with slogans and buttons proclaiming that "Hogs Are Beautiful." And I understand that already they are sold out of buttons.

To amuse ourselves, let us take a look at some of the uncomplimentary terms and phrases being heaped upon the poor pig. Consider these imagemakers, for example:
She is pigheaded.
Her apartment is as dirty as a pigsty.
On weekends, she goes hog wild.
She knows as much about politics as a hog knows about Sunday.
She is always hogging the show.
What's more, she is a road hog.
Her congressman is nothing but a porkbarrel politician who feeds at the government trough.
I've never met her, but they say she is as fat as a pig.
Who wants to buy a pig in a poke.
Maybe she is all lard, who knows?
I've heard rumors that she casts her pearls before swine.
Does she have a cute little piggy bank?
Yes, I know, but you can't make a silk purse out of a sow's ear.
On the dance floor, she is as awkward as a hog on ice.

Scintillating Semantics of Swine Slang

Now that we have a pig's eye image of this girl, how would you like to go whole hog and hire her as a member of your congressional staff?

So much for the scintillating semantics of swine slang. . . .

Yes sir, pigs are versatile creatures—and smart, too. Sometimes they are smarter than we think. For example, I recall a story I heard as a boy on my father's farm in Franklin County, Iowa, about a city slicker from Boston who bought a farm near ours. He wanted to get rich quick raising hogs. For a start he had one sow. He wanted some baby pigs so he loaded his sow into the wheelbarrow and pushed her up the road a couple of miles to the nearest neighbor to visit a boar. Then he wheeled the sow home again. Next morning he went to the barn bright and early, but to his surprise there were no little pigs. So he hoisted the sow into the wheelbarrow and repeated the journey. Next morning he went to the barn again—and still no little pigs. But there was the sow sitting in the wheelbarrow.

Yes sir: pigs are smart. Even Abe Lincoln thought so, for he once said: A pig won't believe anything he can't see.

CHAPTER SEVEN

The Congressman
Plugs His Products

TALL STORY IN THE WINE GLOW

Describing its superior quality is only one way to call attention humorously to a state's products.

To put a point across about the charms of California's wines, that state's Democratic Senator Alan Cranston is forever telling his Soak Oak yarn. It seems at St. Helena, California, there is a three-hundred-year-old tree called the Soak Oak, which grows over the Beringer underground wine cellars, dug a long time ago by Chinese coolies. The tree got real sick. Its leaves took on a rubbery look, and started dropping off. Agricultural experts tried sprays, insecticides, everything. Finally they discovered one of its roots had put itself down into a wine casket. And the root couldn't be simply cut off. Nor could its wine intake be immediately withdrawn. The tree was definitely an alcoholic. It had to be weaned and dried out, allowed a drink of wine for a few hours and given progressively less and less. Today it thrives.

A TOBACCO SPITTING CONTEST

Democratic Representative Gillespie V. Montgomery of Mississippi rose on the floor of the House on August 4, 1971 to tell about a national tobacco spitting contest:

Mr. Speaker, I am happy to announce that the seventeenth annual

TEXAS REPRESENTATIVE JIM WRIGHT ASTRIDE TEXAS BRAHMIN STEER: One House restaurant steak sandwich special coming up. Dev O'Neill Photo

national tobacco spitting contest was held this past Saturday in Smith County, Mississippi, which is located in my district. I had the pleasure of participating in the politicking part of the annual affair but not the actual contests.

The two main events are for accuracy and distance. The distance title was won for the fourth straight year by Don Snyder of Eupora, Mississippi. He managed a distance of 24 feet, 9-1/2 inches. Don set the world's record last year with 25 feet, 10 inches. The accuracy event was won by Mike Thompson of Raleigh, Mississippi, when he hit the bull's eye three consecutive times.

I am told that you need a good pucker and a lot of wind to be proficient in tobacco spitting. I would suggest in good humor that some of my colleagues consider entering the contest next year.

Representative Gene Taylor (R.-Mo.) gives a boost to the fish in his state by describing Nixa Sucker Day:

Mr. Speaker, this weekend, it will be my pleasure to join with thousands of my fellow Missourians, along with countless numbers of tourists in the city of Nixa, Missouri, for the sixteenth annual sucker day celebration.

This event provides one of the finest fish frys that has ever been enjoyed by man, woman, or child. Those who are privileged to attend are fed the succulent yellow sucker, spawned and nurtured in the beautiful Finley River, and cooked to a golden brown in huge kettles right in the heart of town.

Mr. Speaker, the clouds have begun to part and the sun is breaking forth in the heart of the Ozarks in southwest Missouri. The suckers are bountiful, the deep fryers are boiling, and the cooks are ready to go. I guarantee all who attend Nixa Sucker Day a meal that will rank closely to that which was once fed to the multitudes from five little fishes and two loaves of bread. Y'all come.

*　　*　　*

ONE MAN'S ROBES, ANOTHER MAN'S RAGS

In mid-August of 1969, the fashion industry of California was delighted to have their Republican Representative Charles H. Wilson offer on the floor of the House some low-keyed irony about the natural evolution of style in clothes.

Mr. Speaker, the other day my distinguished colleague, Representative Burt L. Talcott [R.] from the great state of California, offered for our enlightenment and edification, a lengthy digest of what is and what is not proper decorum for members of this distinguished body engaged in legislative business within the walls of this chamber. . . .

Would the gentleman suggest that the long tails, high boots, leotards, and wigs of the First United States Congress are now appropriate? I think not. Would the gentleman suggest that the beards, long coats, capes, and tophats of the nineteenth century should still be worn? Again, I would think not. Yet is it not true that if some member at some time had not walked onto this floor attired in a slightly different, somewhat modified progressive style from what was presently popular, we would today still be standing here, powdered, wigged, belted, and booted in precisely the same manner as our Founding Fathers? Probably so. And is it not true that if some forward-looking legislator had not once shown the imagination and courage to take a step forward in fashion we would be standing on the Capitol steps in today's high temperature roasting and boiling in long black coats and tophats? I should think so.

In Hardtop Wearing a Tophat

To those courageous souls who battled the forces of sameness and regimentation, we owe a deep debt of gratitude. Where would we be today if we went to dinner in Georgetown dressed like Thomas Jefferson? Probably mistaken for the doorman at an early American discotheque. What would happen if we slid into a sleek 1969 hardtop wearing a tophat? It would doubtlessly have to be collapsible.

My point here is not to suggest that my distinguished colleague is ready to ease the members of this body into a time machine for a journey back to antebellum. My point is a simple one: If individualism and the courage to be different are to be decried by those who sit in this chamber, we had better pack up and call it a day. Why bother to have a Congress at all if the individualism upon which this nation was founded is condemned within these very walls? What would visitors think if they came to the galleries and saw 435 identically dressed men sitting in a row? They would probably decide to give up voting—what is the difference, they would reason.

Now I am by no means venturing the opinion that dignity, taste, and proper manners should be dumped in favor of a ball-park atmosphere; not at all. But dignity takes many forms. Why, just recently, the President

of the United States attended a state dinner in the Philippines dressed in
an embroidered silk shirt, proving that the fabric of diplomacy is not al-
ways woven from the threads of a dark blue suit. And suppose the sturdy
residents of the North Pole became the population of a fifty-first state.
Clearly, they would be most likely to send to the Congress their most
popular leading resident—how would Santa Claus look clean shaven,
coming down the chimney in a dark blue suit? And what of our attractive
female colleagues who share this great chamber with us? I daresay
"dark business suits, plain, light-colored shirts and dark single-colored
shoes" would not do much for them; not much at all. In other words "to
each his own" or "one man's robes can be another man's rags," if I may
alter an old axiom.

The distinguished gentleman [Mr. Talcott] being from the State of
California as I am, should pause to consider the great leadership our
state has exercised in many important areas. One of these areas is the
realm of modern, attractive, up-to-date fashions, which have led the way
for the rest of the country. . . .

TO SPARK EFFECTIVE LEGISLATION

Representative Charles E. Chamberlain (R-Mich.), known in some
quarters as the automobile horn of Congress, because of his long vocal
opposition to the automobile excise tax, gave his own plug for the A.C.
Spark Plug, made in Flint, Michigan in his district. When the Congress
convened one January he presented each of his colleagues with a spark
plug, and told them the beginning of the session is a good time for members to have their spark plugs checked or replaced.

I trust the spark plug fits the cylinder of your mental, as well as your
high-powered combustion, engine. It should ignite the cerebral mixture
within, and carry an electric current to spark effective and brilliant leg-
islation on the floor of the Senate and House during the coming session.

Being well-designed, this spark plug meets with the following re-
quirements:

1. Provide the proper spark gap . . . whether a hot rod investigat-
ing type, or a spacemobilator who spends his mornings out of this world,
it should ignite motors smoothly.

2. Run at such a temperature as not to cause pre-ignition . . . will
keep you from getting so hot that voters will think you're running for Pres-
ident . . . that is, unless you are.

3. Operate without fouling . . . built-in resistors are useful.

4. Operate without radio and television interference . . . this requires real sharp spark!

5. Operate without failure in rarefied atmospheres . . . helpful when beauty queens are orbiting, or on a congressional trip to Venus.

6. Be gas tight . . . prevents windiness on the floor, or in the Record.

7. Small size and low weight . . . sometimes hard to achieve because of banquet circuit and potlucks.

8. Easy to service . . . gotta be available to people from home.

9. Economical to produce . . . especially important in campaign years.

Yours for a sparked up year ahead. And oh yes . . . my own plug for the hometown . . . A.C. Spark Plug is in Flint, Michigan's Sixth District, which I represent. If this plug isn't your size, it also meets specifications for a paperweight.

BROADEN THE SENATORIAL GIRTH

When he was in the upper house, former Republican Senator Charles Potter of Michigan presented a bag of his state's beans to each of his colleagues. Their reactions plus a few yarns were great to springboard a speech.

Senator Mike Monroney of Oklahoma said he admired Potter's courage in sending so rich a food in all the things that will broaden the senatorial girth. Senator Robert Kerr, also from Oklahoma, assured him there couldn't be a more nutritious dish if it were combined with Oklahoma's energy abounding sorghum. Senator Saltonstall of Massachusetts wasn't sure they would compare with Boston beans. Senator Allen Ellender of Louisiana got in a plug for his state product on the back of the bean, by suggesting that anyone who hasn't eaten dried Navy beans cooked long and slowly with a good hunk of salt pork, and served over steamed Louisiana rice, hadn't lived.

Senator Potter usually closed the speech with a favorite story. He said the reason the people of Michigan were so select and so ingenious in the automobile business and in manufacturing was because of the lake winds and the Michigan beans. Persons of weak lungs were soon cut off by the lake winds, and those of weak stomachs were killed early by the Michigan beans. Michigan folks were a survival of the fittest.

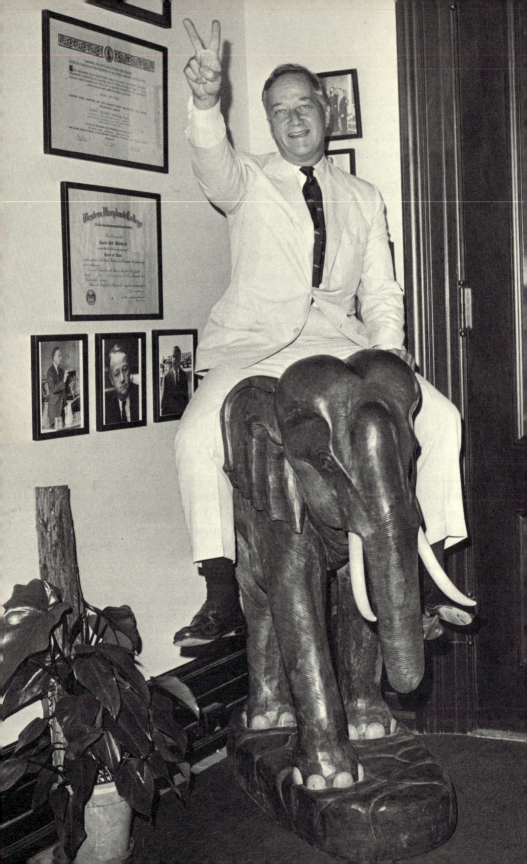

CHAPTER EIGHT

The Politics of Animals

PORKY TELLS IT LIKE IT IS

Members of Congress also indulge in a variation of the politics of humor simulating the stories of Aesop, La Fontaine, and Chandler Harris in his Uncle Remus tales. They use personification and amusing yarns about living creatures other than man, to illustrate a legislative point, to springboard what could otherwise be a dull speech, or to clarify something for their constituents.

Some of these yarns run short and to the point.

A favorite animal story with which Democratic Representative Bertram Podell of New York often begins a more serious speech on voter responsibility, is about a pig and a chicken walking down a street. When they pass a restaurant advertising ham and eggs for 65 cents, the chicken says to the pig, "Porky, looka there . . . see the great contribution we are making to feeding the human race. We're really the greatest, old Piggy Boy."

The pig only grunts in reply.

Then they pass another eatery, displaying a sign in the window saying, "Bacon and Eggs, 85 cents."

The chicken says, "Porky fella, there's more evidence of the same thing. I don't know how the human race would feed itself without us."

Again the pig only grunts in reply.

Then the two pass still another bistro. This time a western omelette is prominently advertised for 99 cents, and the chicken says, "There you

SENATOR CHARLES MC C. MATHIAS: Some call it political burlesque.
Senate Republican Policy Committee Photo

have it again, Porky. You know what's in that western omelette . . . mostly you and me."

This time the pig stops walking, and says to his companion, "Look, Chicken, I'm sick of your boasting and bragging about what you've contributed to feeding the human race. All you give is a quick flip of your bottom. I give my all."

SEE HOW EFFECTIVE MY DUST IS

Certain federal agencies continue when their further usefulness has become a matter of controversy. Every year they surface to public attention, when they need further appropriations. At the end of May, 1972, the week before the Subversive Activities Control Board came to the House of Representatives for its money, Democratic Representative Sidney R. Yates of Illinois told a story about a commuter on a Long Island Railroad. The fellow was surprised to see a man across the aisle dipping his fingers into his empty hat, and then waving his hands in a sprinkling motion through the air. The commuter asked what he was doing. The man said he was scattering anti-tiger dust over the train to keep the tigers away.

The commuter protested that there were no tigers within thousands of miles of the place.

"Ah," exclaimed the man, "now you see how effective my dust is."

Employees of dust-sprinkling agencies avoid Representative Yates.

SEAGULL: A CAPITALISTIC BIRD

Democratic Senator William J. Fulbright of Arkansas is one of the intellectual wits on Capitol Hill. In 1963, before Jonathan Livingston Seagull was born, the chairman of the Senate Foreign Relations Committee brought to the floor of the Senate his thinking on Jonathan's forebears:

Mr. President, I recently came across an article in National Wildlife magazine on the mores and mating habits of sea gulls. My initial reaction to the article was that I had learned somewhat more about sea gulls than I really cared to know, but on further reflection I realized that I was manifesting the rather stuffy and superior attitude which we humans all too often direct at our inarticulate fellow creatures.

The sea gull in fact is a marvelous bird. Unlike many other species, it is entirely free of socialistic tendencies. It is in fact a capitalist bird, a rugged individualist with a highly developed regard for the sanctity of private property. Every family of sea gulls has its own nesting land, about seven feet square, and the family estate is absolutely inviolable. To invade one of these private preserves is the gravest of offenses, punishable by swift and stern retaliation.

In addition to his sound economic doctrine, the sea gull is guided by rigorous standards of morality in his private life. Courting is conducted with dignity and ceremony, and once wed, the sea gull is monogamous and devoted to family. Divorce is unknown and scandals of the sort which rock great empires in the world of men are considered by sea gulls to be in unacceptably bad taste.

Stretched Neck a Status Symbol

More impressive still is the high regard which sea gull society holds for the principle of seniority. Every gullery has its venerated senior citizens, newcomers working their way up, and a few members whom everybody is allowed to pick on. Under the seniority system the young chick is required to keep his neck tucked in because a high head and a stretched neck is a status symbol among gulls. Nothing is more infuriating to an adult than the sight of a juvenile with his neck stuck out. This is the ultimate in presumption, and the bumptious youngster who holds his head high is likely to be struck dead by an adult who sees him. Where, Mr. President, outside a gullery and the United States Senate, is the principle of seniority more faithfully observed?

The most ingenious and civilized of sea gull folkways are the rules of chivalrous combat. A head held high is the most heinous of offenses, but so long as a gull holds his neck in, he is immune from attack, even if he invades the private property of another bird. The tucked in head is a permanently available form of diplomatic immunity, sacred and inviolable. There is no real equivalent to it in human society except for certain rather limited forms of political asylum for heretics and dissenters. Surely with our superior mental endowment we humans ought to be able to devise a form of protection for our free thinkers and dissenters as safe and as convenient as the pulled-in neck.

When sea gulls do actually fight, they seldom go beyond ceremonial expressions of hostility. When two enemies face each other, they are likely to stand puffing out their wings until one or the other commits the ultimate provocation of leaning over and pulling grass. So terrifying is this act that most fights usually end at this point. Only the gravest of conflicts actually reaches the point of whacking and biting.

Suitable for the Mindless Seagull

It takes little imagination to conceive of the benefits which would accrue to humanity if we were able to apply such civilized techniques to our own rivalries. Pulling grass hardly seems an appropriate expression of hostility for so elevated a creature as man, but certainly we should be able to devise more suitable forms of ceremonial combat. Consider, for example, the battle of Agincourt. It would have been almost as exciting and a great deal safer if the English had tipped their arrows with suction cups instead of sharp metal points.

Or consider the hydrogen bomb. Wouldn't it be a fine thing if we could agree with the Russians to replace all our nuclear bombs with smoke bombs—huge smoke bombs which could set off immense unradio-active mushroom clouds and even make a tremendous noise but do so without a lethal explosion. Surely it is not beyond the genius of modern science to invent such a weapon, one which would permit us the fun and excitement of nuclear war without getting killed.

But all this, I suppose, is idle nonsense, suitable enough for the mindless sea gull but hardly worthy of the most exalted of God's creatures. . . .

*   *   *

Sometimes a member of Congress is carried away by his analogies with other living creatures. He becomes drunk with his own metaphor. In this comment on the floor of the House of Representatives, Republican Representative Paul Findley of Illinois protested about the henocide in certain proposed legislation in which the Secretary of Agriculture could mandate a reduction in laying fowl.

HENOCIDE AFOOT

A fowl deed is about to take wing in the United States Senate. A bill to kill off mother hens by the thousands—maybe millions—is fluttering around the Committee on Agriculture and Forestry.

And pity of pities, all the flapping about it so far has been on behalf of those monied barons in the egg industry who must see profit in the blood of slaughtered hens. Henocide it is called.

They demand that government take the blame for mandating the death of defenseless hens—hens in the prime of motherhood, no less.

If you read the bill itself, you'll probably be like the little boy in the chicken yard who dropped the bubble gum he was chewing. He was confused.

But plucked down to bare facts, the henocide bill is nothing more than a scheme to use the lethal authority of government to force up the market price of eggs by killing hens.

When the truth is out, the villains will flock to cover.

Ugly Ultimate in Male Chauvinism

Imagine the cluckings Ralph Nader and his Raiders will give forth when they hear of henocide. But loud as may be these cluckings, they will be smothered to nothing in feather-flying fury when gals of the Women's Lib discover this ugly ultimate in male chauvinism. They will surely ungirdle their sharpest clawings for those who would slaughter only female chickens—doing nothing, not even harmless, painless vasectomy to the males, the real perpetrators of production.

Surely, they will bare their beaks and demand roostercide instead of henocide.

If, despite Nader's Raiders, Women's Lib, and common sense, the dastardly deed is done, who will come out on top? The eggopoly, of course. About 400 giant firms will, they think, be better off, and the rest of us will have egg on our face.

In truth, the bill would set up an eggopoly able to get the Feds to man the chopping block with penalties of violators set at $5,000 a cackle. With antitrust immunity, the eggopoly could engage in a premeditated conspiracy to raise consumer prices with hardly any fuss and feathers.

Happily for hens, the Senate Agriculture Committee adjourned Monday for lack of quorum. Next try is scheduled for Thursday.

The Congress would be feather-brained to pass the bill. It is a chicken-hearted concoction by bird barons who would scratch out a few extra pennies from the agony of motherhood. If they had any gizzard at all, they would take care of their own troubles with grit—and with no ifs, ands and Butz!

*   *   *

A few weeks later Republican Senator Hugh Scott of Pennsylvania had something to say in less verbiage about farmers being forced to kill hens:

I don't know what the impact will be of what we're doing. The object seems to be to raise the price of eggs. It's the Old Sick Chicken Case. We haven't any party position on eggs. It's too close to Easter. But we do *seem to be close to telling the farmer how many chickens he can raise. The way it was described was "adequate, but not excessive." It shows we don't know what is enough of anything. That's why I asked the other day . . . what is enough?*

DEAD BEES POLLINATE PRIVATE POCKETBOOKS

In the spring of 1972 Democratic Representative Silvio O. Conte of Massachusetts went equally metaphorically and analogically wild as he wove irony and bee-imagery into his remarks on how the taxpayer gets stung.

. . . The Supplemental Appropriations Bill we are considering . . . contains funding for a program that just about has to be the ultimate in governmental ineptitude.

Believe it or not we are paying beekeepers for dead bees. What is worse, we are paying beekeepers for dead bees that were supposedly killed by federally-approved pesticide control activity.

Mr. Chairman, this program should have us all buzzing. If you will excuse the expression, I might suggest that it could lead us to break out in hives.

You may think I am making too much of a small thing, but when I look at the amount of the claims submitted under this Beekeeper Indemnity Program, I can understand why our constituents often suspect us of having bats in our belfry—or, more appropriately in this case, bees in our bonnet. We have created a monstrosity—a real honey of a grab bag.

At present, twenty-eight beekeepers are filing claims, each of which total $100,000. At a maximum of $20 per destroyed hive, that's a lot of dead bees. The beekeeper blessed with the largest quantity of dead bees appears to be Jim's Valley Apiaries of Sunnyside, Washington. He has submitted claims for over one and a half million dollars over the past five years.

Some people may consider the beekeeper's profession to be a dangerous one, but in this case it's the taxpayer who's getting stung.

I imagine our friend Jim out in Sunnyside walks around singing the 1968 song entitled "Honeybee." The words go something like this:

"Honeybee, honeybee,
Won't you be my honeybee
Honeybee, honeybee,
Sweet as sugar candy to me."

I imagine he sings a little louder when he reaches the line:
> *"Take me honeybee*
> *From my misery."*

Exorbitant Prices for Bees' Corpses

According to the claims Jim has submitted for the past five years, he has lost a minimum of 12,937 hives from pesticide activity each year for the past five years. I would think that the administrator of the program would be just a little suspicious over such claims.

. . . Even if we assume for the sake of argument that the claims were based on an accurate count of bee corpses, how do we know that the bees died from pesticides? Mr. Frick testified that they had not even checked on the cause of death to justify the claims. If bees die in an area where pesticides are used, we pay for them—all of them. Apparently, in these areas bees can only die from one cause. . . .

Of course, we should protect our honey bees, but I hardly think we are protecting them by paying exorbitant prices for their corpses.

Bees are important. Live ones pollinate crops. It now appears that dead ones pollinate private pocketbooks.

A GRASSHOPPER HOPS IT UP

Several Congresses ago, a certain member was forever trying to tack a lottery amendment on every bill introduced in the House of Representatives. When he was latching it on to some very technical legislation on banking, Democratic Representative Richard T. Hanna of California countered with these remarks on the floor:

The gentleman's amendment and rationale behind it remind me of the following story: There was a young scientist who was completely wrapped up in his work. One day he invited his fellow workers to come and see his experiment. They all went into his laboratory, where there was a grasshopper in a box, with a speaker inside and wires that led to a microphone. The scientist picked up the microphone and told his friends to watch.

He turned on the microphone and said: "Hop."

The grasshopper hopped.

Nobody was impressed, and the scientist said, "Wait a minute. I'm not finished yet."

He opened the box, tore off two of the grasshopper's legs, put him back in, and again picked up the microphone and said, "Hop."

The grasshopper did the best he could minus two legs, managing a fairly decent hop.

Still no one was impressed. So the scientist took the grasshopper out of the box and pulled off all of its legs, replaced him, picked up the microphone, and said, "Hop."

The grasshopper just lay there.

The scientist said: "See. I've just proved that when a grasshopper loses its legs, it loses his hearing."

The gentleman's amendment is a grasshopper amendment.

*   *   *

Republican Representative Gilbert Gude of Maryland likes to tell a story about Bible times when the rains came, and a pair of giraffes were talking to a pair of elephants and they decided to go look for the ark. Pretty soon they were followed by horses, dogs, cats, bears and deer, all two by two. The line got longer and longer as it approached where the ark was supposed to be docked. But when the animals reached the spot, all they found were two termites. The giraffes piped up and asked, "Hey termites, where's the ark?" And the Termites answered in a big, deep voice, "We can't believe we ate the who-o-o-ole thing!"

IN A CURIOUS FIVE-SIDED HOUSE

Other animal yarns used by members of Congress in their pursuit of the politics of humor ramble on in leisurely fashion. This one by Democratic Representative Jim Wright of Texas sums up a turning point in the nation's military history. Secretary of Defense Robert McNamara, formerly of General Motors, was using his industrial management expertise to get the ordnance buying of all the military services under one purchasing department.

Once upon a time, in a fair and beautiful land where many animals lived, there stood a curious five-sided house. It nestled alongside a broad river in a big and majestic city.

In this house lived a mule, a goat, and a falcon. To them the other animals of the land had entrusted the job of protecting their country from an angry red bear which snorted the kind of fire from which the sun is made and, on occasion, thumped his shoe upon the table.

The mule, the goat, and the falcon all were anxious to protect the land, but among themselves they were very quarrelsome. Each had his own idea on how to defeat the red bear in case he should attack.

"I shall meet him on the land, and with my great mobility and fire-power, I shall kick him to death," brayed the mule, flecking a bit of lint from his forest green suit.

"Tut, tut, there will be no need of that," sneered the goat, who was resplendent in his dark blue suit with gold stripes. "My specialty is the sea, and if the bear ever threatens our shores, I shall butt him right out of the water."

"Nonsense," jeered the falcon, proudly displaying the silver wings on his light blue suit. "If the bear should attack, I shall fly to his home-land, peck out his eyes and destroy his ability to fight."

So it went for many years, with the three animals incessantly bicker-ing among themselves.

The Donkey's Braying and Elephant's Trumpeting

Nowhere did these arguments cause more concern than on a gentle hill which lay just across the river. Here lived a great herd of donkeys and elephants. Even though they themselves were not immune from petty jealousies, they realized there was a desperate need to eliminate the tumult within the great five-sided house. After the donkeys had done much braying and the elephants had done much trumpeting, they decided that another animal should be chosen to take complete charge of the occupants of the five-sided house.

Now it happened that in a large white house not far from the hill there lived an eagle. It was decided to let the eagle choose the animal to be in charge of the five-sided house, provided, of course, that the donkeys and the elephants approved of the eagle's choice.

Many years passed, and several different eagles moved in and out of the large white house. Each eagle chose an animal to live in the five-sided house. Alas, however, the mule, the goat, and the falcon never really stopped their bickering. They seemed to resent every animal that was put in charge of them, and each continued to go pretty much his own way.

Finally one day a new eagle moved into the large white house. This eagle had some very definite ideas about the animal that should be put in charge of the five-sided house. He wanted a wise, but young, owl.

The Animals on the Hill Generally Approved

It so happened that just such an owl lived in a busy city to the west. This owl made a living by providing engines to be used in crossing narrow inlets on the shore of a large lake—the fjord motor company, some animals called it.

The owl consented to take charge of the five-sided house, and the animals on the hill generally approved.

"He's very nice," nodded the donkeys.

"And he can bring to the house the valuable cost-cutting lessons he learned in private enterprise," trumpeted the elephants.

Soon after moving into the five-sided house the owl discovered that the goat and the falcon were planning to buy new swords. Separate kinds, of course.

"Why can't you both buy the same type of sword and save money?" the owl asked.

"That's quite impossible," said the goat with a patronizing smile. "Yes, quite," agreed the falcon. When the owl asked why, the goat tried to explain.

"You see, my sword is to be used at sea," he said. "I have always bought a sword shaped sort of like a 'T'."

"And my sword," put in the falcon, "is to be used for the air and must have something of an 'F' shape."

The wise young owl pulled a slide rule out from under his wing and appeared quite thoughtful. "Perhaps an 'X' shaped sword might serve you both," he observed. "We could call it the TFX, and it would save a billion dollars."

The Owl Who Gives a Hoot

Panic gripped the goat and the falcon.

"It won't work!" cried one.

"It's never been done before!" shrieked the other.

The owl consulted his slide rule again. "Nevertheless I think we should try it. Even though the TFX might not exactly suit your individual preferences, I will promise you that it will provide a far better sword than either of you now has."

Crestfallen and bitter, the goat and the falcon left the owl.

"Whatever shall we do?" cried the goat.

"We shall march straight to the hill and complain to our powerful friends," said the falcon. "One of the donkeys is a particularly close friend of mine."

The goat appeared puzzled. "But aren't the elephants and the donkeys on the hill also very close friends of the owl?" he asked.

"They have been," the falcon gloated. "But they may change their minds if we tell them that the owl is robbing us of an effective means of protecting the country, and that it would be cheaper and better to build two different swords."

"But is that true?" demanded the goat.

"Sure it is," smirked the falcon, winking and nudging the goat in the ribs. "Sure it is."

Moral: As long as we're going to have an owl, we ought to believe in him because he seems to be the only one who gives a hoot.

When Democratic Representative Robert Grier Stephens of Georgia thinks he may have dished too much information in a serious speech, he ends the talk with a penguin story.

A father gave his little boy a book on penguins. Several days later he asked his son if he'd read the book. The boy said he had. The father then asked how he liked it. The boy answered, "All right, but it told me more about penguins than I want to know."

*　　*　　*

And when former Democratic Representative Andrew Jacobs of Indianapolis wants to wrap it up, he says:

A wise old owl sat in an oak.
The more he saw, the less he spoke.
The less he spoke, the more he heard.
Why can't we be like that wise old bird?

CHAPTER NINE

Letters Are Great for Laughs

WHY DO YOU NEED A HORSE?

Some members of Congress write caustic letters to constituents or to somebody else, and then use them in subsequent speeches.

When Mrs. Jackie Kennedy (Onassis) was presented with a bay gelding by President Ayub Khan, it was flown, from Pakistan in an Air Force plane; and former Democratic Senator Stephen M. Young of Ohio, received this letter from a constituent:

Dear Senator Young: I have read in various publications that since Army transports return from overseas positions, it costs nothing to transport horses for citizens of the United States. As for example, there is Mrs. Kennedy's horse, which was given to her. At that time it was explained that the transportation was of no cost.

I have considered an opportunity to buy some foreign horses and wonder if you would furnish a schedule of free transportation back to the United States, so that I might avail myself of this opportunity.

Senator Young replied as follows:

Dear Sir: Acknowledging your letter wherein you insult the wife of our President, am wondering why you need a horse when there is already one jackass at your address. Sincerely yours.

SOME CRACKPOT USING YOUR NAME

To another constituent, who was opposed to socialized medicine, Senator Young wrote:

SENATOR EDMUND MUSKIE OF MAINE (right) TO PEGGY WHEDON (ABC) AND SENATOR HUBERT HUMPHREY OF MINNESOTA: Did you hear the one about the wire a senator sent in response to his constituent's complaining telegram: "Go soak your head in a barrel. Strong letter follows."
Dev O'Neill Photo

Am sending you a letter received this morning, evidently from some crackpot who used your name. I think you will try to protect your name else this jerk will sign your name to other vicious and stupid statements.

* * *

On October 4, 1968, a man in Virginia wrote a page and a half letter to Senator Young which read partially as follows:

Dear Senator Young: I have read a letter in the October issue of The American Rifleman *sent to you by one of your Columbus constituents, concerning your anti-gun views. I have also read your answer to his letter. Some of the phrases in your reply have surely appeared in the wrong letter. . . .*

In your answer to the gentleman's letter you referred to him as a "liar" and a "stupid fool." These opinions were forwarded because his opinion differed from yours, and without a shred of evidence to support either charge. This surely brands you as the stupid fool.

As for the snake's tail in the wagon rut, I am sure you could walk upright, under that snake's tail, with your hat on and have plenty of headroom.

My telephone number is . . . . It will cost none of the taxpayers' money to call me, and I would welcome the opportunity to have intercourse with you. Sincerely:

The Senator answered:

Sir: You wrote me a most insulting letter.

Noting your offer, in the final paragraph of your letter, "I would welcome the opportunity to have intercourse with you," no indeed, I will have nothing whatever to do with you. You go ahead and have intercourse with yourself. Stephen M. Young.

* * *

About two years ago a constituent wrote to Democratic Representative Ray Taylor of North Carolina and complained that the State Highway Commission was failing to maintain the road to a rural cemetery in his neighborhood. The man said this puzzled him because the state maintained roads to other cemeteries. He concluded by saying that apparently the reason the state would not maintain the road to the particular cemetery was that most of the people buried there were Republicans. Representative Taylor's reply suggested the constituent contact the State Highway Commission and he himself would help him in any way he could because he objected to discrimination against dead Republicans—it was the live ones that caused him trouble.

GO SOAK YOUR HEAD IN A BARREL

Senator Robert Byrd interlarded an epistolary note to his politics of humor at a dinner in April of 1971. He said a lady wrote asking him to have the phone company take the telephone poles off the street in front of her picture window. Another sent a letter wanting to know if he could have her husband sent to sea for the duration of the war. He also said a small boy wrote asking for a picture of the Senator and his family. The West Virginia Democrat sent one that had the Byrd dog in it as well. The boy wrote back saying he liked the picture of the Senator and his family, but could he, please, have a picture of the dog by himself.

"Well, we got a picture of the dog and sent that," Byrd added. "And then the boy wrote again. This time he asked if I would send him the dog!"

*   *   *

And still in the letter writing groove, Republican Representative Craig Hosmer of California tells a yarn about a wire a senator, just re-elected for a six-year term, sent to a complaining constituent's telegram: "Go soak your head in a barrel. Strong letter follows."

*   *   *

A windfall of epistolary humor for use in his speeches came to Republican Senator Peter H. Dominick of Colorado when he received a "Dear Peter" letter by mistake from Democratic presidential nominee Senator George McGovern of South Dakota on October 3, 1972:

Dear Peter: I know of the help you have already given me in this crucial effort, but I am writing this note to ask for your additional cooperation in the closing weeks of the campaign.

If you can give any time for speaking engagements in your state or elsewhere around the country, Sarge Shriver and I will greatly appreciate it. Please have your staff contact Stanley Greigg, Deputy of National Campaign Chairman Lawrence F. O'Brien, at 1910 K Street, N.W. 872-1479.

With best personal regards, I am sincerely yours, George.

The Third Consecutive Fumble

The Republican Senator sent a "Dear George" answer to Democrat McGovern:

Dear George: I certainly appreciate your letter of October 3, thanking me for the help I've given and asking that I give additional time for speaking around the country.

As Chairman of the Senate Republican Campaign Committee, I am happy to tell you that I have been in New Mexico, Wyoming, Illinois, Michigan, Oklahoma, Texas, California, Colorado, Virginia, Florida and other states in the past six weeks, and every time I mention your candidacy, it brings quite a reaction—somewhat like the Philadelphia Eagle fans greeting their team after the third consecutive fumble.

It is also nice to know that you have me in mind, and although I was not able to respond with financial support to the three letters I've had from Ted Kennedy on your behalf, it is reassuring to know that your staff still does its customary fine investigative work.

Be assured that I'm trying my best to be 1000% behind you.

Best personal regards: Sincerely, Peter H. Dominick, United States Senator.

TAKE OFF FOR THE HOG PENS

Former Democratic Representative Andy Jacobs of Indiana last year participated in a much publicized floor debate on the war in Vietnam. He received a post card from Gary, Indiana, which said bluntly that the Indiana congressman was an incompetent jerk. Jacobs replied: "Sir: Thank you for the kind compliment. Naturally I should dislike being a competent jerk."

Representative Jacobs also tells about a letter exchange in an earlier, more earthy congressional era. A constituent wrote: "Sir—if I ever find myself in your presence, I will take off for the hog pens." The congressman answered: "Sir: It is okay by me, but why put off visiting your kin folks?"

SENATOR HENRY JACKSON OF WASHINGTON: A presidential candidate needs perfect balance.
Seattle Times Photo

CHAPTER TEN

Senator Jackson Back on Campus

THE WALL-EYED REUNION STARE

As with successful people in any profession, some members of Congress go back to their universities years later and tell their former classmates what the world looks like through their bifocals. Senator Henry M. Jackson, Democrat of Washington, returned to the thirty-fifth reunion of his law school at the University of Washington, in the spring of 1970, to say these among other things:

Politicians are creatures of habit and no politician worth his salt makes a move without taking a poll. When my invitation to this event arrived in the mail, I ran a quick survey and found that six out of ten otherwise stable persons have, at some time in the past five years, toyed with the idea of attending a class reunion. Three out of ten had not toyed, and one had no opinion of toying. Obviously the fellow was not a lawyer.

Two of the six, it should be noted, actually went. From the beginning their worst fears were realized. A series of endless encounters with familiar faces and forgotten names was not helped too much by the distribution of name tags—which only contributed to a wall-eyed reunion stare, one eye attempting a friendly focus on the classmate's face while the other tried to bring the name into view in the right section of the bifocals. But a politician is supposed to rise above those hazards, so I decided to come anyway. . . .

In the currently popular book, The Godfather, a story of the Mafia, the Mafia chief is giving advice to a young orphan he has raised and is about to send him off to college.

"Be a lawyer," he tells the boy. "A lawyer with a brief case can steal more money than our whole family with pistols."

Just to take revenge, I intend to follow the Senate rules here tonight. This is to say that my remarks will be both lengthy and irrelevant. Senators, you know, are past masters of oratory, which is best defined as the art of making deep noises from the chest sound like important messages from the brain.

Perhaps the organizers of this function thought I needed a safe forum after being pelted with marshmallows during recent speeches in such diverse places as Mankato, Minnesota, and Pullman, Washington. I like to think it was all planned, and had nothing to do with the quality of the speeches. My staff tells me it was all the work of a militant marshmallow minority!

Senator Thurmond's Anti-Ballistic Marshmallow

In any event, I can report that the marshmallow brigade in our home state was a lot better organized than the group in Minnesota. Our native marshmallows were stale—which makes a harder missile—and were covered with terse comments for my benefit. I won't go into the details of these comments but one of the marshmallows had an "X" rating. I've got Senator Thurmond working on an ABM—an anti-ballistic marshmallow.

The right to privacy is one of our most cherished constitutional rights. In this electronic age, when snooping has become a fine art, only constant vigilance will preserve this basic right. For this reason, I want to comment tonight on one of the most flagrant invasions of the right to privacy I have ever encountered. I refer, of course to the so-called 1935 Law Class Census and Questionnaire mailed to each member of this class.

After thirty years in public life, I have not fought for the Fifth Amendment for nothing. On this questionnaire, I intend to take it.

My reluctance to deal with these questions frankly reminds me of the two Czechoslovakian citizens standing on a street corner in Prague. Two automobiles, an American Ford and a Russian Moskvitch, stopped at the traffic light.

The first Czech answered, "Well, I like the Moskvitch."

"You don't know your automobiles," the first man said.

"I know my automobiles but I don't know you," the Czech replied.

Well, I do know the members of this class and there are just enough Republicans in the crowd to make me wonder about how this questionnaire might be used later this year.

As Fat or Bald as the Rest of Them

I have no fear, of course, about the questions which ask about personal appearance. Unfortunately, on this count, the facts speak for themselves. It's been said that after age fifty, a man has to take responsibility for the face he presents to the world. As I look around tonight, I can only say that some of us have a lot of responsibility.

The question is: In comparison with the other members of the class do you regard yourself as: [1] Younger looking .... [2] Older looking .... [3] About as fat or bald as the rest of them ....

Really, now. I regard myself in the same way everybody else does — from my 1952 campaign picture.

As for the question asking us to pick our best law school professor, what politician of sound mind is going to pick one and lose forty votes in the process?

I admit to being intrigued by the question that asks what and who prevented you from having better grades than you received when you were in law school. Well, actually, I didn't get married until 1961.

Here's an interesting one: As you reflect upon your law school career, can you recollect any incident involving yourself or others that should now be fully revealed at the reunion? Specify?

I have frankly racked my mind on that one, and the only thing I can come up with is the blood oath I took at the time with some people who have since assumed charge of the Washington State Republican Finance Committee.

After thirty-five years of calculated cover-up, we are asked to tell all. Some of you may feel moved to respond. I will only note the remark of an obscure British statesman who said that the proper memory for a politician is one that knows what to remember — and what to forget.

The Generation Gap and Nudity on Stage

But the most scandalous questions of all appear on the last page of the questionnaire where we are casually asked to record our attitude on various subjects which are innocently described as "present day matters of controversy." The first item on the list is sex. Having already taken a firm stand on birth control, I am in trouble enough with the Archbishop.

ILLINOIS SENATOR CHARLES PERCY: I didn't do so well in Latin eith
Joe Melena, Menlo Park Recorder Ph

This attempt to draw me out on the subject of sex is an obvious effort to undermine my political career.

As for such topics as the generation gap and nudity on the stage, I am glad to respond that those matters are not within my jurisdiction as a United States Senator!

As for the subjects of pornography and the Supreme Court, I am willing to concede that they are controversial. It has been argued that we should have less of one and more of the other, but which is not entirely clear. As a possible candidate for public office in the future, I will reserve my position until the issues are clarified by public debate.

On the subject of the Supreme Court, however, Gerry Ford and the Republicans are currently making an effort to impeach Justice Douglas. But the Democrats cannot believe that they are serious.

Can you imagine this administration trying to fill two Supreme Court vacancies?

Another question asks about my memberships, and the associations I have held over the years.

Jokes from Coast to Coast

I'm really not much of a joiner, but I've tried to maintain my membership in the Shriners, Knights of Columbus, Leif Erickson Society, the Swedish Club, the Sons of Italy, and B'nai B'rith. Additionally I've earned another small distinction—I'm a lifetime Boy Scout.

As I look at you tonight, I recall the famous remark of Edward Everett Hale, Chaplain of the Senate. He was once asked: "Do you pray for the senators, Dr. Hale?" The Chaplain answered: "No, I look at the senators and pray for the country."[1]

After thirty-five years, as I see the members of the Class of 1935 before me tonight, I am silently praying for the profession.

Thank you very much.

---

[1] Democratic Senator Sam Ervin also uses this joke in speeches in his native state of North Carolina. The jokes on Capitol Hill get around from coast to coast.

REPRESENTATIVE BELLA (THE HAT) ABZUG: What I want is a Women's Lib Cheeseburger to eat at my desk. What do I mean by that? Equal cheese and equal beef.
Photos by Betsy K. Frampton

CHAPTER ELEVEN

Steinem Sending Poison Pen Letters

HIS WIFE NOW CARRYING A GUN

Women's libbing and related topics intermittently surface as a target for congressional humor.

At the January, 1973 congressional dinner of the Washington Press Club, William D. Hathaway, the new Democratic Senator from Maine and a former member of the House of Representatives, used his win over Senator Margaret Chase Smith to springboard some political fun. He said the people of his state were giving him a hard time on his recent victory:

A woman called me up after the election and said, "Well, I voted for you, but you didn't have to win."

I called my mother and told her I beat Margaret Smith, and she said, "You ought to be ashamed of yourself."

My wife is now carrying a gun, my daughter is circulating a recall petition, my sister's been kicked out of women's lib.

I've alienated all the older people, of course all the women, and everybody by the name of Smith, not to mention the Boy Scouts of America and the horticulturalists. The Defense Department has asked me to give back my good conduct medal.

Gloria Steinem is sending me poison pen letters. I don't know why Mrs. Smith is in hiding, but it certainly couldn't be because she's mad at me. I sent her a telegram the night before the election saying that I hoped the better man would win.

JUNE ALLYSON A BRIGADIER GENERAL

In 1957 former Senator Margaret Chase Smith herself raised questions about Jimmy Stewart's training deficiency and lack of activity in the Air Force Reserve when he was nominated for promotion to Brigadier General. In a discussion with the then Secretary of the Air Force and the Air Force Chief of Staff, the opinion was expressed that Stewart rated being made a Brigadier General on the basis of his lead role in the movie *Strategic Air Command.*

Senator Smith's response to this argument was one of incredulity. She said, "You do not really seriously believe Jimmy Stewart rates a Brigadier Generalship for playing in a movie for which he was undoubtedly paid at least several hundred thousand dollars? That surely cannot be considered Reserve duty and participation!"

When the answer was a vigorous, decidedly positive, "Yes," Senator Smith countered with, "Then why don't you make June Allyson a Brigadier General for playing the female lead in *Strategic Air Command!"*

*   *   *

Senator Edward Kennedy of Massachusetts had this to say at the Gridiron Club Dinner in the spring of 1971, when he walked through picketing women to get into the hotel where it was held:

As you know, many of your guests tonight had some misgivings about attending because of the outspoken opposition from the ladies. I talked to some of my colleagues to see how they were going to handle the situation.

George McGovern said straight out that the dinner was discriminatory and he wouldn't attend.

Hubert Humphrey said he'd be pleased as punch to attend, as long as he could be out in time to do "Face the Nation," "Meet the Press," and "Issues and Answers"—and perhaps shake a few hands down at the Greyhound bus station.

Scoop Jackson said he'd come if he could sit with the Joint Chiefs of Staff.

Harold Hughes told me he'd be happy to attend, and asked if he could deliver the invocation.

When I asked Ed Muskie, he took the longest time to reply. He considered the arguments of the women's group. And then he pondered the prestige of the Gridiron Club. And finally he made his decision—he'd attend, but he'd only stay for half the dinner.

As for myself, I had accepted this invitation over a year ago. And if

Bella Abzug calls, just tell her what I told her this afternoon—I'm spending a quiet evening at home.

LIKE EVANS CONVERTING NOVAK

A year later the ladies were marching again outside the hotel, where the Gridiron Club's dinner was held. Republican Representative Margaret M. Heckler of Massachusetts had been asked to speak, and said a funny thing happened to her on the way to the Statler Hilton.

> *Somebody outside carrying a sign asked me, "What's a nice girl like you doing in a place like this?"*
>
> *I told them I just play piano and don't know what's going on upstairs.*
>
> *They still tried to dissuade me from coming in and attempted to convert me.*
>
> *That's a little like Evans converting Novak.*
>
> *The messages on the placards were interesting. I especially liked the one that said, "Trust in God for She Is Good."*
>
> *The women journalists assured me they don't want to be like men. All they want is access—to the Gridiron and to Jack Anderson's sources. What turned them on was news of his latest column in which he asks, "Did Clifford Irving write the Beard Memo?"*
>
> *I told them I'm really here to help them. Actually, I'd rather be inside sticking the needle in your conscience than outside getting splinters in my hand.*
>
> *So here I am. And if I play the piano, it won't all be the theme from Love Story.*
>
> *It's more likely to be a medly of tunes by that great composer, Nicholas Chauvin.*

Nicholas and His Chauvinists

> *He too had a musical group more popular than the Washington Gridiron Club. It was called Nicholas and his Chauvinists.*
>
> *Of course, I didn't know this was to be a completely musical evening.*
>
> *I thought there would be an opening chorus of "Anything You Can Do, I Can Do Better," and that would be that.*
>
> *. . . Tonight's point lies in the story of a housewife.*
>
> *She went down to her basement one day wearing nothing but curlers and a housecoat. She was throwing dirty clothes into the washing machine and decided the housecoat was dirty too. So she took that off and threw it in.*

As she stood in front of the washing machine, some water pipes overhead began dripping on her hair curlers. Looking around for something to protect her coiffure, she spied her son's football helmet and put it on. And there she stood, in the altogether, wearing only a football helmet. Just then, she heard a noise behind her. Turning around, to her horror she discovered the gas man reading the meter.

He took one look at her and said, "Gee, lady, I hope your team wins."

He could have said a lot of things. But he struck the theme, I think, of all this tonight, inside the hotel and outside, inside the Gridiron and outside. We all ought to think about what he said, and maybe play the game a little fairer.

NO UGLIES BEHIND RENT-A-CAR COUNTERS

In the spring of 1972, when women's rights flared up as a political and social issue, Democratic Representative William L. Hungate of Missouri had some serious comments to offer on the subject:

The most vicious form of job discrimination today is not against women as women. It is against one group of very unlucky women—ugly women. The women I mean are not just "plain" or "unpretty." I'm talking about those whose faces are ill-favored, whose figures are unshapely, whose general appearance is unappealing. Women such as these are brutally discriminated against by employers.

Now, this is a very difficult problem to discuss. You can't even bring up the subject with its victims.

Yet, it's there. Just glance through the "Help Wanted" columns of any newspaper. Note how many ads specify "attractive" or "a nice appearance" or "must be able to meet the public." It's a widespread method of discrimination—so common that most of us don't even notice it.

Have you ever seen a fat or ugly woman behind a rent-a-car counter? Have you ever found an over-forty, ugly woman in an airline stewardess' uniform?

In government too, the lower-paying Civil Service jobs have a noticeably higher proportion of homely girls than the higher-paying ones do. Ugly women not only get fewer jobs, but lower-paying ones as well. How many women would be capable of saying, "I'm ugly—and I've lost out on a job because of it?" Anyone who tried to recruit members to an Association of Ugly Women to fight for their rights would probably get his face slapped for his efforts.

CHAPTER TWELVE

Congress Is Articulate on Cabbages and Kings

NEVER SEEN RAYMOND BURR STAND UP

And, of course, not a session of Congress goes by without some member taking a humorous swing at some aspect of the media, a government agency, the Post Office Department, the military, or bureaucratic language.

Among other things, Senator Robert Byrd, Democrat of West Virginia, had this to say about television on the floor of the Senate on September 20, 1971:

Mr. President: . . . America has just endured the first week of television's new offerings. . . . A full twenty of the fifty-six prime time hours of our three major networks are occupied by detective shows—blind detectives, fat detectives, private detectives, and detectives upholding the honor of local, state, and federal governments.

If our streets were as amply patrolled as our prime time television hours, we could all sleep a lot better at night.

To be certain, it is not important that an entire generation which is now maturing has never seen Raymond Burr stand up. But I think it is important that Americans are coming to expect nothing better than mediocrity from television—that they are beginning to feel that the best the networks can do is to copy from each other. One network creates "Bonanza," and Americans have only to wait one season before prosperous ranchers settle down on the other two major networks. That kind of programming, Mr. President, can hardly be applauded.

NATE MINORITY LEADER HUGH SCOTT OF PENNSYLVANIA: I don't want to y anything else. I put my toe in the water here (on Capitol Hill) and my tail gets in ot water downtown (The White House).
Official Senate Photo

Guests Scheduled on a Shotgun Basis

. . . *Given the television fare as it is today, practically any interruption is enjoyable.*

This does not have to be the case. Most Americans would welcome quality programming. One has only to consider the reaction to "The Six Wives of Henry VIII" to know that.

. . . *It is true that American history had no Henry VIII, but anyone with even a passing knowledge of American history would concede that there is material aplenty, of high dramatic content, which would enliven our television screens.*

. . . *And not just in the field of drama. Talk shows, for example, are now marked by a sameness that makes watching them more a testament to the viewer's boredom than to the program's content. One network sits the host behind a desk. Another network will place its host in a swivel chair and consider this a meaningful change in programming. Directors for most talk shows seem to think that scheduling commercials for low phosphate detergents during an appearance by an ecologist constitutes a significant contribution to our way of life.*

With rare exceptions, guests are scheduled on a shotgun basis—an ecologist is followed by an acid rock band that uses enough electricity to light up a city—and few of the interesting guests are given a sufficient amount of time. There even have been occasions where the main guest on one talk show has been the host of another talk show. . . .

ONE FELLER'S SMELLER NOT THE NEXT FELLER'S SMELLER

On November 12, 1972, Representative B. F. Sisk (D-Calif.) took a few verbal shots at the Environmental Protection Agency:

Now would you like to be a government sniffer? A "G-Nose," so to speak? I hasten to say that I am not recruiting—as far as I know, there is no such job just yet. But there may be. And if there ever is such a thing as a G-Nose, it will be because of the Clean Air Act of 1970 which makes creating a bad smell a legal offense.

When it comes to measuring how bad a smell is, science cannot provide either standards or a measuring device. But the Environmental Protection Agency has a legal duty to come up with both. Other types of pollution are fairly easy to measure because they can be stated in physical or chemical terms. In sound, there is the decibel level, and there are instruments to measure it. In water, there are instruments to measure how many parts per million are present, of various individual chemicals and of specific combinations. The same holds true in air pollution generally. But smell? No way.

Smell is a personal sense and is known to vary widely in different individuals. Smells that offend some people are considered a rare treat by others. For instance, there is a perfume oil on the market presently at extremely high prices. Some persons are willing to pay those high prices because they consider the scent exotic and sophisticated. Others — including some of the sellers — say "It stinks!"

You may recall an old advertising slogan, "Your nose knows." It's true, but only as to you — not to anybody else. You are the only one who can say whether a smell is good or bad to you.

So whose nose is going to be the judge as to whether an industrial plant, or a feed lot, or a hog farm, or a winery pond, or whatever else, is polluting the air with a "bad smell"? EPA is trying to come up with an answer. And one of the suggestions is to use official federal sniffers.

What Is an Odor Unit?

Sometime in November, EPA is expected to propose regulations under which a local official could draw a flask of supposedly offensive emissions and submit it to a panel of eight sniffers. Seated in a bare room and breathing charcoal filtered air, the panel would sniff various dilutions of the sample and decide whether the plant had exceeded the ceiling for stench — say two hundred "odor units." This would determine whether the plant would have to clean up. But what is an "odor unit?" How does one panel member's idea of an odor unit square up with that of a person seated next to him? And how do you assure that both members sniff in exactly the same amount of air at exactly the same rate? Wouldn't the last member be sniffing a less-concentrated sample? And in the long run, it all boils down to the fact that "one feller's smeller's not the next feller's smeller." I think any attempt to designate such a procedure as "scientific" is just downright silly.

EPA hasn't asked me, but I have a suggestion. Instead of setting up a pseudo-scientific method, why don't we revert to commonsense, democratic methods? By that, I mean, why not let the persons who live nearest the source decide the question. If, for instance, two-thirds of the people who live within a mile of the source say it is creating a stench — why not take their word for it? Maybe a mile isn't the right distance. Maybe two-thirds isn't the right majority. But surely something worked out along these lines has a better chance of standing up in court than some fake-science method.

Shucks, there was a lot of G-Nose jobs "with the wind." But if I know EPA, it will stick with its present intentions. So if you hanker to be an official sniffer, just wait awhile.

OUR GOBBLEDY-GOOKISH LANGUAGE

Representative Omar Burleson (D-Tex.), in the spring of 1972, took off on language that tells it twisted like it isn't:

. . . We are reminded of a sign in the museum at the head office of the Union Pacific Railroad in Omaha, Nebraska. A faded photo of the sign stuck up along the right-of-way somewhere in Nebraska or Wyoming about a century ago reads: "NOTIS, trespassers will be persecuted to the full extent of 2 mongrel dogs which never was over sochible to strangers and 1 dubble brl shot gun which ain't loaded with sofa pillers. Damn if I ain't getting tired of this hell raisin on my place. B. Griscom."

Of course, Mr. Griscom has long departed this life but he leaves a simplicity needed in our gobbledy-gookish language of today, found particularly in government. . . .

A Dead Mackerel in the Moonlight

The Bible has a way of making things pretty clear. "Go to the ant, thou sluggard," says Proverbs. Sluggards are now "underachievers." No one cheats any more. Rather he is "ethically disoriented."

Genesis says that the people of Sodom "were wicked and sinners before the Lord exceedingly." This is pretty tough talk, so modern sociologists prefer to describe the Sodomites as having a deviant life-style, a confused behavioral pattern, and maybe an alcoholic subculture.

Restraints and refinements are desirable, but they were a little less observed in the nineteenth century when Senator Beveridge was told that a corrupt politician should at least be given credit for gracious manners and a brilliant mind. His response was, "Yes, and like a dead mackerel in the moonlight, he shines and stinks and stinks and shines."

Another good one we often hear now is an "unmet need" which means anything a public official wants to spend money for. People who demand things they are not willing to work for and gain for themselves are exhibiting "rising expectations."

On and on it goes. The kid who hangs around a tough gang is now *suffering from "an identity crisis and driven to seek the supportive approval of his peer group." This often excuses him from looting coin boxes, swiping cars, and maybe right on up to robbing the First National Bank.*

There used to be hobos and bums. Hobos drew the distinction that they would work when they were hungry but bums would not. In modern references hobos are "itinerants" and bums are people suffering from "motivational deficiencies due to deprivation."

AMBUSHES IN ROME, A MASSACRE IN PARIS

After the tragic events at the Olympics in 1972, Representative Burleson had this to say about violence and crime in general:

Floods, storms, war, holdups, unprovoked and irrational assassinations, such as occurred at the Olympics, are brought to us immediately by instant communication. The notion of these being uniquely bad times may not be entirely true.

Imagine, for example, a sixteenth-century existence with television and the daily papers across our nation offering global coverage of news.

On a typical day in that time one might have had breakfast to reports and commentaries on witchcraft in the Carpathians, a hari-kari wave in Yeddo, ambushes in Rome, a massacre in Paris, treason charges against English Jesuits, carnage among Araucanians, and a Mogul penetration in India. In the sixteenth century there wre abductions, conspiracies, piracy, plague, and atrocities. In the period of the Islamic Empire, cruel rule was imposed on two-thirds of the then civilized population of the world.

With instant coverage, knowledge of such adversities would have reached those comparative few immediately affected. Even then it was probably a considerable time after such happenings before there was much known about them. It can be reasonably supposed that the shock of the act was dulled to the point that today's exclamations, "Something must be done!" or "We can't let that continue!" were not used. . . .

*   *   *

In 1965 during a debate on Medicare, Democratic Representative Frank Thompson, Jr., of New Jersey suggested a modest tax proposal to help doctors.

HOUSE-CALLERS ANONYMOUS

Thompson said he had a plan for these poor neglected, downtrodden servants of society. He called his program Doctorcare.

"Doctorcare would be financed by a 2 percent federal sales tax on apples, apple juice, applesauce and apple pie. It's foolproof—the more apples people eat to keep doctors away, the more the doctors benefit! Either way, they can't lose," Thompson said.

He planned to use Doctorcare funds to finance a telephone answering service for doctors. Although cynics may dispute it, he claimed it was still possible in some areas of the country to call a doctor's office and speak with the doctor. He said this had to stop if doctors were to have time to do any serious thinking about caring for the elderly.

The New Jersey Democrat also proposed that Doctorcare funds be used to establish "House-Callers Anonymous." It would operate like Alcoholics Anonymous. Its purpose would be to help doctors who cannot resist a plea for a house call. He said the organization would function like this.

"When a member feels an overwhelming temptation to make a house call, he would immediately dial a secret number. A recorded voice would say: 'Get hold of yourself! You're a doctor—patients come to you. Only television repairmen, milkmen, and paper boys make house calls. Don't lose your grip!'"

If this failed Thompson said the doctor could dial another secret number. Two doctors would immediately come to his office and rush him off to a Cadillac showroom or a golf course to help the backslider overcome his weakness. Doctorcare would pay the caddies, greens fees, and mahjong losses.

"But that isn't all Doctorcare would do," Thompson noted. "Funds could also be used to promote research in specialization. Why, for example, should an eye, ear, and nose man be required to know everything? If we had 'right ear men' and 'left ear men,' our ears and the profession would flourish."

He said if Doctorcare worked as well as he thought it would, perhaps it could be merged later with Lawyercare. This, of course, would be financed by a 2 percent federal tax on ambulance sirens.

"This seems logical," Thompson added. "So many lawyers practice medicine and so many doctors are constitutional lawyers, they really should join forces. But enough for Lawyercare for the moment. That will have to await the results of our anticipated battle with the Apple Growers' Lobby."

*   *   *

Republican Senator Frank E. Moss of Utah had this to say about unnecessary expenditures on the Senate floor:

Every election year, as regularly as the cherry blossoms and a good deal more punctually, a great number of people who want to get elected to public office—or who want to get someone else out of public office—set out to slay the dragon of unnecessary public spending. Fortunately, he is an out-of-town dragon. He never lives in your own state or in your own congressional district. He comes from someplace else, and he has no constituents. If you represent a midwestern constituency, he is down South putting wasteful price supports under peanuts and cotton and tobacco; if you live in the South, he is way out West building shipyards that will put the next three generations of southerners in debt. Or, if you live in the past, he is burning up the taxpayers' money on schools and on medical care for old people who did not plan ahead.

Unnecessary government spending does not have many real friends, but he does have quite a few casual acquaintances who are willing to go out on the town with him so long as nobody from home sees them together.

*   *   *

A story about the glow of the vine is always good, and the members of Congress are no exception in telling them.

Republican Representative Craig Hosmer of California tells about a legislator running for re-election who complained that his scurrilous opponent was accusing him of being a drunk. A helpful colleague offered to give him an affidavit stating that, "I've seen you sober quite a few times."

Former House Majority Leader Hale Boggs referred to the difficult task of compromise and persuasion on the House floor to form majorities as the Art of the Possible, and illustrated it often with this story:

Two drunks woke up one morning across the street from a barroom. One turned to the other and said, "Boy, I sure do need a drink." The other replied, "So do I, but how do we get one when we don't have any money."

The first said, "Well, I'm going in that barroom over there and get one."

So he goes in, walks up to the bar, and orders a double bourbon on the rocks. The bartender pours it, the drunk gulps it down. Then the bartender tells him "That will be four bits." The drunk says indignantly, "What do you mean four bits, I paid you already."

Whereupon the bartender says, "Oh, I am sorry, buddy. I don't know what has gotten into me lately but I haven't been myself. The old lady has been complaining and the heater went out at home. Please excuse me."

VICE PRESIDENT SPIRO AGNEW: I like to have the press where I can keep my hands on it.

Karl Shumacher Photo

CHAPTER THIRTEEN

Goldwater, Fascist Gun in the West

WASHINGTON POST CALLS HIM NEANDERTHAL

Speeches before social clubs give members of Congress a forum to indulge in the politics of humor.

Senator Barry Goldwater of Arizona gave this talk at the Alfalfa Club Dinner on January 23, 1971, in Washington. Alfalfans are a group of prominent men in the nation's capital, who intermittently nominate a candidate for President, and he is usually selected from among the famous losers of national elections.

Mr. Vice President, Mr. Chairman, My Favorite Congressmen, Friends and Fellow Members of the Alfalfa Party:

You are to be congratulated. You have made the perfect selection. I am the ideal candidate. I have had experience. I have had an audience with the Pope. I have talked with Golda Meir. I have visited the Wailing Wall. I have been to Vietnam. The New York Times Encyclopedia has me listed as a Democrat. The Senate Clerk calls me a Republican. Bill Buckley's National Review calls me a Conservative. And the Washington Post calls me a Neanderthal.

I start off with twenty-seven million votes. I want to prove I can lose some of those.

But I am really just an Episcopalian who is restricted to playing nine holes on Gentile golf courses because I am half Jewish.

Don't think that because I was presented here tonight by Congressman Barry Goldwater, Jr., that we have begun a political dynasty in the far West. We refuse to preempt Massachusetts' claim to that political course.

I mentioned experience. Gentlemen of the Alfalfa Party, I really have it. I am the only man who has been nominated for President on three different occasions—twice by the Alfalfa Party and once, in 1964, by a splinter group which called itself the Republican Party. Experience is important. Look what it has done for the seniority system in the House and Senate. And, of course, anyone who has been number two as often as I have is bound to try harder. I haven't met a soul who voted against me in '64—I am considering a recount.

Grew Up to Become Arizona's Alf Landon

Although I am hip deep in experience, none of this has gone to my head. I'm still that shy, retiring, barefoot boy from Phoenix who was born in a log cabin and grew up to become Arizona's Alf Landon. But now I know all the pitfalls of politics. In fact, I dug most of them myself.

While the honor you bestow is not new, I appreciate it. In my heart, I know you are right. And in my heart I know Mike Mansfield will be happy to look out over the Senate and see at least one presidential candidate who isn't a Democrat.

On the Senate—a few more candidates and we will never get a quorum.

By the way, since his defeat for Democratic Whip, I hear Ted Kennedy may run for President under an assumed name. And Ed Muskie is trying hard to be another Lincoln. In fact, he's wearing the same kinds of suits. You'll notice when Muskie gets up, his pants don't get up with him.

Among Republican possibilities, my friend Ronnie Reagan faces a big decision. He can't decide whether he was born in a log cabin or a manger.

Needless to say, I plan a vigorous all-out, "shoot-from-the-hip" campaign tailored after the battle I waged for Lyndon Johnson in 1964. I don't think anyone can doubt I got more votes for old LBJ than anyone else on his team.

After all, extremism in the pursuit of votes is no vice, and moderation in the pursuit of money is no virtue.

I have been called an extremist. That's not quite true. I only go to extremes when I'm arranging my own defeat.

And as for shooting from the hip, Westerners aren't acquainted with any other style. Wild Bill Hickock, Billy the Kid, Johnny Ringo, Butch Cassidy, and John Wayne all cut loose from that part of the anatomy. I followed their example and I am now known as the "Fascist gun in the West."

Another thing my campaign will do will be to provide the voters of this country with a clear-cut echo of everything that was said in 1964 and absolutely no choice at all. I tried the other way around. I offered a choice, not an echo, and everyone chose my opponent.

So this time the choice is out and the echo is in.

But I'm used to cliff-hangers like the one in 1964, and of course, everyone expects me to turn back the clock in true reactionary fashion.

Sex Education Back in the Drive-In Theatres

I hope you realize my first big task will be to find a "household word" to run with me as a candidate for Vice President. The last time out Congressman Bill Miller was my running mate. I made an elder statesman of him in a hurry. I don't remember what he looked like, but I know he was wild. Candidates are easy to forget. But this will never happen to Spiro. If the public ever forgets him, every comedy show on television will fold up and a whole army of gag writers will have to go back to work.

I may ask my friend Hubert to run with me. If I do, I can promise him he can trust me—I will stand behind him—empty handed.

. . . In my campaign I shall lay great stress on one of the prime forces in our society. My reference is to sex. I have noticed the only military volunteers we get nowadays went to sign up for service in the sexual revolution. In this same connection, I would urge a program to take sex education out of the schools and put it back where it belongs—in the drive-in theaters.

You know, sex is a lot like politics. You don't have to be good at it to enjoy it. People have asked me what I think of sex in the streets. Well, it may be one of the newer ways to demonstrate against the establishment, but it's got to be damned uncomfortable.

. . . The generation gap will get plenty of attention from the Alfalfa Administration. Frankly, I am not at all sure that the kids aren't out to get us. Now that we've given the eighteen-year-olds the vote, I hear they're trying to use it to deny the vote to everyone over thirty. Sometimes I wish we could turn back the clock to 1933 when all we had to fear was fear itself.

. . . *I have given much thought to the selection of a Cabinet.* . . . *First off, let me say I plan to add a Department of Hunger, and my choice for Secretary of Hunger would be Senator George McGovern. I don't think there is anyone on the national scene who is more "for hunger" than that former bomber pilot, George. He bombed Europe—now he bombs the SST.*

For Secretary of the Interior I plan to name my defeated opponent, Ed Muskie. We need an ecologist in this job who is determined to take pollution out of all the streams in the nation that don't run through the State of Maine.

For Secretary of Defense, I am leaning toward Senator William Proxmire of Wisconsin. I tend to favor him because of well-founded reports that he is in favor of a new "super-tonic slingshot" to replace our present military deterrent capability and for his constant defense of a strong military and a stronger Military-Industrial Complex.

Saw Off the East and Let It Float Away

There can be only one logical choice for Secretary of Agriculture and that is Mr. Cesar Chavez, the darling of the California grape and lettuce growers.

Selection of a Secretary of State has caused me great soul searching. . . . *I feel these times cry out for the gentle, diplomatic touch of Martha Mitchell.*

Now, if I wanted to go the rough and tough route on this appointment, I would of course name Senator Bill Fulbright. His job would be to utilize his facility for brow-beating the Communists to negotiate a new agreement with the Soviet Union. We need something in writing which would permit us to disarm unilaterally without interference from the Communist Bloc.

. . . *Now just a word about campaign strategy. I will have no Southern strategy; but I will have an Eastern one—saw it off and let it float away.* . . .

*   *   *

On January 24, 1970, Senator Hubert H. Humphrey of Minnesota was the mock presidential candidate at the Alfalfa Club.

Mr. Vice President, President Byrd, Secretary Rogers, and President Johnson, wherever you are. . . . *Gentlemen of the Alfalfa Club and guests:* . . . *before we proceed on this historic convention: I am no longer a household word. My distinguished successor is.*

> *. . . It is strange, but somehow I can't believe this is a real nomination. Where's Dick Daley? Where's the tear gas? Where's Gene McCarthy? Where's Sandy Vanocur?*

> *And no one seems mad at me! There are no policemen, no hippies, no yippies, not even any Eastern television commentators with smirks. You can always tell those fellows by their smirks.*

Nixon Eating Ketchup and Cottage Cheese

I didn't really make up my mind about your nomination until I drove past the White House today and realized that for a whole year Richard Nixon has been sitting in there, eating ketchup and cottage cheese, watching football games, and telling everyone that he represented the silent majority.

That really got me mad. What the Alfalfa Club needs is someone who can out-Nixon Nixon. I said to myself, "I've eaten more cottage cheese than he has, I've been to more football games, and God knows I have been silent for a majority of my public career."

> *. . . You've heard a lot of stories about campaigning, but let me tell you what it was like. Here's a typical day—*

First thing in the morning, a guy from Dale Carnegie hit me in the nose.

At noon, a guy (and that's a guy, not goy) from the Anti-Defamation League called me a dirty ethnic name. Later I got on an elevator and someone tried to hijack it to Cuba.

Before dinner, I called Dial-a-Prayer and they hung up on me. . . .

A year ago when I found myself out of a job I did what everybody else does. I went down to the unemployment office and filled out the forms. The interviewer asked me some questions.

Humphrey, a Restless Job-Hopper

"Well, Mr. Humphrey, what kind of a job do you feel qualified for?"

"President of the United States," I replied.

And he wrote down, "Needs intense counseling."

Then he asked me how long I had my last job and I said, "Four years."

"You mean to tell me, Mr. Humphrey, that you're fifty-seven and you've been on your last job only four years?"

So he wrote, "Restless job-hopper."

Then he asked for references.

I said, "How about my ex-boss?"

"That's a fine reference. What does he do?"

"Oh, he's out of a job, too."

So he suggested I go back to college—and that's what I have done. It's great to be working with students again. The other day they locked themselves in my office and wrote dirty words on the wall—Dent, Birch, Chotiner, Mollenhoff, Mitchell, Thurmond.

An Instinct for the Windpipe

. . . Remember, some nasty commentators said that Richard Nixon—who deserted the Alfalfa Party when success reared its ugly head—once had an instinct for the jugular.

Well they're the same people—the very same people—who say I have an instinct for the windpipe.

. . . Even the drinking habits have changed in Washington. When I was carrying that other banner, everyone drank bourbon and branch water. Now it's Pepsi Cola.

Other things are changing at the White House, too. Everyone is traveling—first class. The Vice President just returned from golfing in Asia and checking the dominoes.

Secretary Rogers is going on an African safari—using Dean Rusk's accumulated vacation time.

And the President himself left California—Watergate West—for a few days visit to the White House East.

. . . After Mr. Agnew made his speech about our unbiased, totally objective media, I called the LBJ ranch.

"Mr. President," I said. (He still likes for me to call him "Mr. President.") "Isn't that terrible the way Vice President Agnew attacked your friends in the press?"

"Who is this?" he shouted softly.

"It's Hubert, Hubert Humphrey, your own man," I said respectfully.

"Oh yes, Mr. Vice President. (I still like for him to call me that.) I heard that speech. Now, there is a Vice President who knows his job."

We can't say that the Republicans are much better off than the Democrats. They have lost the mayoralty of New York—at least I think they did—and Ronald Reagan has ideas again.

New York Garbage Gets into Print

. . . And Spiro Agnew can't be counted out. He just bought his wife a cloth coat. And his brother is already writing a book. And just the other day, the Vice President said, "I know what happens to the eight million pounds of garbage New York puts out on the street each night—they print it."

. . . Let us rally now together, let us reason together—let us lower our voices, let us look past the old politics of Democrat and Republican, to the new politics—the politics of Hi Spirits and Low Resistance—of Alfalfa. We will run on an Alfalfa platform:

—where hay fever will replace the common cold

—where the only grass that is smoked is alfalfa

—where Henry Kissinger will remain in the White House so that our national anthem can be "Whose Kissinger Now"

—when we will hire an Israeli commando unit to move an Egyptian pyramid to Johnson City so that the seventh wonder of the world can rest next to the eighth, God willing and the River Pedernales doesn't rise. . . .

FOR GEORGE MEANY, EBENEZER SCROOGE SCHOOL OF CHARM

The various grades and brands of humor used in the speeches and other oratorical sorties of Vice President Spiro Agnew may, in his position as President of the Senate, also be blanketed into a book on congressional humor.

Mr. Agnew starts many of his serious speeches with a page or two of seasonal political wallops. On December 14, 1971, he began his talk before the United States Association of Life Insurance Counsel in New York City by distributing a few Christmas gifts within the framework of that month's news.

. . . I thought you might be interested in a couple of items on my Christmas gift list:

For George Meany—an introductory lesson at the Ebenezer Scrooge School of Charm.

For Martha Mitchell—a brand new Princess phone.

For John Mitchell—a padlock for a brand new Princess phone.

For President Nixon—in preparation for his trip, a complete history of China.

For Chairman Mao—in preparation for the President's visit, a complete history of the National Football League.

For Ralph Nader—a secret report from Nader's Raiders demonstrating that the human foot is unsafe to walk on.

For Ambassador Bush—so that he can entertain all our friends at the UN, a two-place dinner set.

For Richard Salant, President of CBS News—a new desk with legs cut on the bias so that the documentaries will come out straight.

For the New York Times—Daniel Ellsberg's unlisted telephone.

For Daniel Ellsberg—a lifetime subscription to LOOK magazine.

And finally for the Public Broadcasting Corporation—a collector's item, a piece of video tape which reveals Sander Vanocur in an unguarded moment making an objective statement.

THE WASHINGTON POST PATTERN

A month later speaking at the Touchdown Club in Birmingham, Alabama, Agnew, after a few amenities, started his talk this way:

Thank you for the kind introduction, Mr. Ferguson. Actually, for a group like this, it might have been sufficient to say simply that I'm the fellow from the nation's capital who's been criticized in recent seasons for not running the post pattern very well—that is, the Washington Post pattern.

. . . I welcome the chance to forsake the world of the Chicago Seven and Manhattan Twelve for that of the Alabama Eleven and the Auburn Duo. . . .

You already know that President Nixon is our country's number one football fan. His enthusiasm for the game is contagious.

It's not simply a matter of his putting inspirational messages on the Cabinet Room blackboard: messages like, "Winning isn't everything, but it beats anything with less than a plurality," or "When you send a bill to Congress three things can happen, and two of them are bad."

No, more than that, the President even has his challengers over at the opposition party headquarters thinking in football terms for the 1972 nomination. Just the other day, they tell me, Larry O'Brien had some of the Democratic hopefuls out on the practice field, testing them for the quarterback slot in a triple-option offense.

Ted Kennedy Faked up the Middle

It was really something to see, according to my informants. And very revealing.

For example, George McGovern wanted to pitch out to a trailing back—but couldn't find anyone trailing him.

Scoop Jackson ran into trouble, too. He couldn't find his Florida primary receiver—but he Meanys to keep trying.

George Wallace found he had reported to the wrong team. Coach Larry O'Brien won't even talk to him or show him the play book.

Vance Hartke thought about using a quarterback sneak. But, unfortunately, Jack Anderson was out of town.

Then came Ted Kennedy. He faked up the middle, faked right, faked left—and finally decided to run himself. When he was brought down for no gain, he complained about the condition of the field.

John Lindsay got a turn, too, even though he's a new member of the squad. It was a typical Lindsay performance. First, he changed uniforms. Then he fumbled for a twelve-yard gain. That wasn't too bad, but when the play was called back for clipping, he asked the referee for a general amnesty.

Gene McCarthy went Mayor Lindsay one better. When a demonstrator ran onto the field to break up the practice, he handed him the ball game.

Commentators Know-It-All Monday Morning Quarterbacks

But the biggest disappointment of all was Ed Muskie. He drew a five-yard penalty for taking too much time in the huddle making up his mind. And when Hubert was last heard from, he was still calling an audible at the line of scrimmage.

The practice was covered by ABC sports. But halfway through it they lost the sound portion because of technical difficulty. Howard Cosell dropped his dictionary and it snagged his breakaway jersey.

There are, it would seem, a great many parallels between the world of football and the world of politics.

Coach Bryant and Coach Jordan have their know-it-all Monday morning quarterbacks: They're called alumni.

FRESHMAN SENATOR WILLIAM L. SCOTT OF VIRGINIA (right) TO SENATOR ALAN CRANSTON OF CALIFORNIA: What do I have to do to get that?

CHAPTER FOURTEEN

Congress
Laughs at Itself

WHO GOT THE FURNITURE?

First-person yarns about their own experiences have always played a large role in the politics of humor of members of Congress.

On February 2, 1972, Democratic Representative J. Edward Roush of Indiana described, on the floor of the House, supplies delivered at the door of his district office back home in Indiana:

Mr. Speaker, either the General Services Administration expects me to stay in the Congress for a long, long time, or I have just experienced one of the most hilarious, or ridiculous, things I have ever seen happen.

Mr. Speaker, I have set up a small office back in my district and we have been trying for a year now to get furnishings for that office from the General Services Administration. Some furnishings have been supplied; however, I am still waiting for certain furnishings which were ordered months ago.

Yesterday I talked to the district office and Miss Judy said, "Congressman, you will never believe what has happened. First, you should know that we did not get our furniture. However, the freight office informs me that you have there for delivery the following items: 315 pounds of floor sweeping compound, 155 pounds of cleaning compound, 1,625 pounds of paper toilet seat covers and 1,950 pounds of toilet tissue."

Mr. Speaker, I do not need all of these items.

HONEY CHILD, THE QUEEN OF GREECE

In Greece, in 1960, Democratic Senator John Sparkman of Alabama, introduced himself to the Queen as just that, "Senator John Sparkman."

A colleague said, "You should have said Senator John Sparkman of Alabama," after they had passed the Queen.

The Queen turned around, "Oh! Are you from Alabama?" she asked quickly.

Senator Sparkman said, yes, he was from Alabama.

The Queen then said she had met a young lieutenant recently and he had said, "I'm from Alabama, honey."

The Senator smiled, and said to the Queen, "He should have added the rest . . . honey child."

So the Queen of Greece was called "Honey Child" the rest of the night by everyone at the informal gathering.

* * *

Former Senator Dennis Chavez always said he experienced the greatest personal put down of any member of the Congress. He stood smilingly while the orchestra played for several minutes at a political banquet. The New Mexico Democrat couldn't understand why his wife and his aides looked glum and kept their arms folded, during the whole musical prelude to the dinner.

Then an aide told Chavez why. The orchestra had been playing, "I'll Be Glad When You're Dead, You Rascal You."

* * *

When President Lyndon Johnson was in the Senate, his colleagues and friends kidded him about the slim eighty-seven vote margin which won him his first primary victory. And when they did, he invariably spun this yarn about Juan, a small Mexican-American boy, who was found crying on a street in El Paso. A man asked why he was crying and Juan said it was because his father had come to town the day before and hadn't come to see him. The man looked surprised. "Juan, your father has been dead for a couple of years, you know that."

But the boy didn't stop crying. He said, "My daddy came to town to vote for Lyndon Johnson; then why didn't he come to see me?"

BLACK BOTTOM IN DETROIT

Democratic Representative John Conyers, Jr., of Michigan, in a speech before the Amalgamated Clothing Workers Union in Miami, de-

scribed this incident in connection with a political campaign. The Black congressman had gone back to the first house in which he had lived on the east side of Detroit, and where the photographers wanted to take some pictures.

Nobody here knows where Black Bottom is in Detroit on Sherman Street. We pulled up in several cars. I got in front of this very old house that was still managing to stand up, and the photographer began taking pictures.

Pretty soon some of the gentlemen in the neighborhood began to come around and they were whispering and pointing at me. One of them came up to me and said, "Say, didn't you used to hang around the drugstore on the corner there about twenty years ago or so?"

And I said, "Yes, I did."

He said, "Didn't you and your brother used to play baseball at the Smith Playground in the summertime?"

I said, "That's right."

He said, "And you used to live in that house, right?"

I said, "That's correct."

He says, "I know who you are. You are John Conyers." He said, "Hey, gang, this is John Conyers."

They said, "Yes. He used to live there."

Then he turned to me and he said, "Hey, by the way, what are you doing for yourself these days?"

And I pulled myself together with all the aplomb of a future member of Congress, and I said—well, I'll be very modest about this—I said, "Well, I'm a Federal employee. I work for the government."

He said, "No kidding? You're in the Post Office, too, hey."

PLOTTING A PALACE COUP

Self humor of the one liner variety was occasionally used by the usually serious Senator Robert F. Kennedy, when he was in the upper house. Assigned to a back row seat in the Senate chamber, his comment was that he had better seats for "Hello, Dolly."

And when he was planning a skiing trip with his family and still another person around his Senate office said he was glad the Senator was getting away, Kennedy told the fellow he was the ninth person to say that, and wondered if a palace coup was being plotted.

Before that in his 1964 campaign for the Senate, Kennedy also offered the crowds at rallies a few one liners. When a queue to shake

HORUS OF BLACK CONGRESSMEN: Capitol restaurants gotta' have Soul Food.
Dev O'Neill Photo

hands with him seemed to be growing instead of diminishing, he suggested the people were shaking his hand and then going to the end of the line. And he gave as his reason for worrying about his possible defeat in his try for the Senate, that he didn't want to become a retired elder statesman at thirty-eight.

THE HAT CONFRONTS FISHBAIT

Representative Bella (THE HAT) Abzug (D-N.Y.) told this one about her first days in Congress to the New York Clinical Psychologists on February 26, 1972:

Most of my encounters in Washington have been verbal, with one or two exceptions. When I first came to Congress, I was considered quite a novelty. One reason, I suppose, was that I'm a woman and there are only eleven of us in the entire House. They'd also heard about my very strong views on ending the war and the need for social change, and the rumor had circulated that I sometimes got so impassioned about this that I used four-letter words. One of the wire services carried this completely fabricated story about how I was insisting on wearing my hat on the floor of the House and Fishbait Miller, the official doorkeeper, said I couldn't, and how I then gave him a sexual directive. Completely untrue: I had never even met him. One day I was talking with Carl Albert, the Speaker of the House, and the door opened and this little man about five feet tall came in, stood up on his toes, and kissed me.

"Whoever you are," I said, "I think this is an over-response."

"Oh," he said, "I'm Fishbait Miller and I just wanted to greet you."

We've been very friendly ever since.

WINNIE IN EVERY PUB

Maggie is the nickname of Democratic Senator Warren Magnuson of Washington. He's had this nickname in high school, in college, in the Senate. And sometimes he fits this anecdote about it into a speech:

So I was down at the White House one time. I was invited down. I was very honored, I thought, as a young congressman. And there was a stag dinner down there that Roosevelt was giving for distinguished guests. And Roosevelt, you know, if you knew him, he . . . one of his great, almost a fetish with him, he liked to dominate all the dinner conversations, because to him getting ready for dinner, this was his whole activity at night. All the rest of us, you know, can be running around and he couldn't. So he referred to everybody around the dinner table. There weren't too many people there, maybe 16-18. Some of them by their nicknames, but everytime he mentioned "Maggie"—something like that. So, after the dinner was over we were walking down to the library and the guest of honor came alongside me and put his hand on my shoulder and he said, "Young man, I noticed the President always calls you Maggie. Do you resent that?"

"Oh, no, I don't resent it." What was I going to say?

"Well," he said, "young man if I were you I wouldn't resent it. I really think the reason that I'm Prime Minister of England is I'm known as Winnie in every Pub in the Country."

The nickname never bothered me after that.

* * *

Democratic Representative Robert Grier Stephens of Georgia tells about coming into Georgia and heading for the U-Drive-It agency where he had reserved a car by telephone from Washington. When he arrived, he did not see his name on the bulletin board with people who had asked to have cars ready for them. He inquired about this. The woman at the desk asked his name. He said, "Congressman Robert Stephens." The woman went off somewhere to inquire what happened. When she came back she said it was easily explainable. They simply didn't know whether Congressman was his last or first name. Rather than make a mistake, they decided not to put it up on the board with the others.

* * *

The same congressman says he now has proof of his success.

When the eleventh edition of the *Biographical Directory of the American Congress, 1774-1971* was recently issued, something new had been added.

"All my life, I have been introduced as the great-great nephew of Alexander Hamilton Stephens, vice president of the Confederacy and member of Congress," the congressman says. "The new biography of Vice President Stephens reads: 'Stephens, Alexander Hamilton, great-great uncle of Robert Grier Stephens, Jr.!'"

YOU DON'T LOOK SO HOT IN BLUE EITHER

Representative Glenn R. Davis (R.-Wis.) believes one of the hazards of a politician who moves over campaign trails that have been traveled before is the person who comes up and grabs his hand with the challenge, "I bet you don't know who I am, do you?"

To explain any names the congressman might have himself fluffed or fudged, he often throws this story into a speech:

A candidate was accosted by a female constituent in a remote part of his district and found himself completely taken aback. He had no idea of the identity of the lady. While he floundered, there raced through his mind that tested rule of name identification, the association of the name with some tangible object. In this case, he noted that his challenger was wearing a brown suit, and so in desperation he blurted out, "I can't say that I do, but you do look like Helen Brown." At this point the lady flared up and responded, "Well, you don't look so hot in blue either!"

*   *   *

Republican Senator Robert J. Dole of Kansas was asked if his kidding friendship with the press had anything to do with his hasty removal from his post as Republican National Chairman.

"There was never any question of my leaving. There was just no fixed date for my withdrawal," he answered.

Alluding to his replacement in the post, George Bush of Texas, former Ambassador to the United Nations, he said, "Some say I was pushed. Others say I was bushed. It amounts to the same thing."

NO SIXTEEN BLOCKS TO INTERVENE

Right after President Lyndon Johnson had moved into the White House, the late Senate Minority Leader, Senator Everett Dirksen of Illinois, said his audience should not be misled by the Chief Executive's appearance of taking weight on around the hips and chest. The new President was only doing what he did in the legislative branch—stuffing his pockets with clippings about himself.

On September 2, 1960, around adjournment time, Dirksen said to his colleagues: "I extend to the senators who are candidates the warm hand of fellowship. We want to keep them here. It would be lonesome without my distinguished friend, the Majority Leader Senator Lyndon Johnson, and without my distinguished friend from Massachusetts, Senator John F. Kennedy, with whom it has been my honor and pleasure to work on the Senate Labor Committee. My affection is as high as the sky and it is as deep as the sea—and I do not want sixteen blocks to intervene."

A BRIDGE OVER THE RIVER CRY

When Pennsylvania Republican Senator Hugh Scott was telling

members of the press that Vice President Spiro Agnew had been desig-
nated by the President as the go-between to whom members of Congress
might come when they had a quarrel with the White House, he added,
"You know, something like a bridge over the River Cry."

*   *   *

After Democratic Senator Allen Ellender of Louisiana died some
months ago, a note was found in his files. It read, "If there is a life
hereafter, I want to come back as a standing subcommittee in the Senate,
because they never fade out."

The Democrat from Louisiana had been a great foe of the prolifera-
tion of needless subcommittees and their staffs.

*   *   *

After he fended off 150 attempts to amend the 1964 income-tax reduction bill, one of his colleagues commended the skillful performance of
Senator Russell Long this way:

If a man murdered a crippled, enfeebled orphan at high noon on the
public square in the plain view of a thousand people, I am convinced
after today's performance that, if the Senator from Louisiana represented the guilty murderer, the jury would not only find the murderer in-
nocent, they would award the defendant a million dollars on the grounds
that the victim had provoked him.

*   *   *

And a famous verbal tilt between the Democrat from Louisiana and
the late Minority Leader Everett Dirksen, is one of the great practical
jokes of the upper house annals. Some years ago, Long noted there were
no Republicans on the floor during a debate. He immediately asked for
unanimous consent to abolish the Republican Party. The next day Dirksen
retaliated by asking for unanimous consent to abolish the state of Louisiana. However, Senator Long had heard via several grapevines what
Dirksen intended. He stepped on to the Senate floor stage from the wings
of the Democratic cloakroom, and objected.

*   *   *

A couple of favorite stories used in speeches by Democratic Representative Claude Pepper of Florida, who was once a member of the Senate, tell about two of the most colorful actors on the Senate stage.

Last year Pepper was speaking to the racing commission in Miami,
when some of the things his crime committee was uncovering about its
members had leaked to the press. He needed to soothe his audience, so he

began by saying it was a pleasure and honor for him to be there, and they should remember it was a criminal offense to lynch a congressman. Then he told the following story:

Democratic Senator Alvin Barkley of Kentucky was at the track, when a man smacking his lips came up to the pari-mutuel window. He bet $1,000 on Bluebell and went away. Later he returned to bet another $1,000. When he came a third time and bet the same amount, Barkley asked how he could bet so much on Bluebell. He said he knew Bluebell. He was slow. He couldn't possibly win. The man answered with enthusiasm, "Oh yes, he can. I own the other four horses."

THE BOTTLE IN THE CORNER CUPBOARD

The other story was one Democratic Senator Tom Heflin of Alabama told when Republican Senator William Borah of Idaho kept declaiming on the Senate floor that he did not want an increase in his senatorial salary. Heflin said he was reminded of a Kentucky gentleman with a weakness for his state's famous Bourbon. He lay in bed very ill. One day about sunset, he felt himself becoming increasingly weaker. He looked out of the window at the shadows of the trees growing long on the beautiful blue grass outside, with the closing of the day. The gentleman beckoned to his wife and said, "Dear, will you go down in the cellar and bring up that bottle in the corner cupboard. Take a tall glass and put some ice in it, pour a drink into it, and fix me up a real long drink. Then go over to the kitchen window, where there's that mint you have growing there. Break sprigs of the mint into the drink and hang a piece of the green over the edge. See that there is a lovely frosting on the outside of the glass."

He was beginning to lose his breath, but he managed to finish what he had to say.

"Then, dear, bring it here to my bedside, and whether I want to or not, make me drink it."

*   *   *

During Representative Richard T. Hanna's first congressional campaign in 1962, former President Truman came to California to help him. At a dinner honoring the Democrat, he introduced everyone on the podium with him. When he came to President Truman, he said: "And of course we all know our great former President, President Hoover!"

HOW THE OTHERS GOT THERE

Republican Representative Craig Hosmer of California says that during one of his re-election campaigns, he made quite a speech, and afterward an old fellow told him, "Son, I like what you say, I'll vote for you. Golly, anything would be better than that congressman we've got now."

*   *   *

He also says the first year in Congress the member wonders how he got there. The next year he wonders how the rest of them got there.

*   *   *

Democratic Representative Wayne Hays of Ohio wasn't so sure his party wanted to perform as a political umbrella to include Republican Donald W. Riegle of Michigan. On February 20 of this year he rose on the floor of the House of Representatives to say:

Mr. Speaker, I want to implore the Republican side of the House—I do not see the gentleman from Michigan on the floor—however, I want to implore the Republican side of the House to try to dissuade him from switching parties. We in the majority have treated you fellows pretty nice since I have been here, so I do not see why you would want to inflict him upon us. You know, after all is said and done, we have enough troubles of our own, and I do not think you ought to send any of your troubles over on our side.

We had a couple of switches around here a few years ago, one notably from South Carolina, and somebody said at that time the Lord giveth and the Lord taketh away, blessed be the name of the Lord.

Well, this time I just hope, since the Lord has given him to you, that He keeps him over there and you do all you can to keep him there, too.

*   *   *

Former Senator Kenneth Keating of New York, at a dinner given by the Washington Press Club, had something to say about the prominent Democrats of the turn of the 1959-60 decade. He said Lyndon Johnson figured the best road to the White House was the Milky Way. He was the first man to try to turn outer space into a congressional district. About Senator John F. Kennedy, he said, "Jack has problems. Every time he appears on a TV panel show, thousands of viewers write in to ask which college won the debate."

He noted that Adlai Stevenson "still leads most of the Democratic polls. This shows Democrats have no desire to ruin the sport of the thing by any compulsive urge to win."

He also said Hubert Humphrey is the first man to run for President on the basis of spending eight hours to answer a simple question. His talk with Khrushchev, he understood, was to be made into a movie called the Lynx and the Larynx.

Taxpayer a Vanishing Race

And Keating summed up the Democrats this way, "I've heard it said that there's only one real difference between the Democrats and Republicans. A Democrat says things are awful and tells a joke to cheer you up. A Republican says things are wonderful—and then weeps at the beauty of it. Actually I prefer another definition. We Republicans think of a person first as a taxpayer. The Democrats think of a person first as a voter. Obviously the voters are increasing by leaps and bounds—while the taxpayers are a vanishing race. So how can you win?"

* * *

Republican Senator Norris Cotton of New Hampshire tells this one on his colleagues in the upper house. An elderly lady in the visitors' gallery heard the quorum bells. She asked a page why they were ringing so urgently. The young man said he wasn't sure. Then, gesturing down at the Senate chamber, he added, "Maybe one of them has escaped."

* * *

And once when Senator Cotton was asked what he thought the Senate would do on spending, he said the members were in such a mood that if a senator introduced the Ten Commandments, the upper house would cut them down to eight.

CAPITOL DOME LIT FOR HANKY PANKY

Republican Congressman John Schmitz of California says members of Congress will do anything to keep their seats.

There is the ego appeal, for instance, in which they are invited to very important meetings, where their pictures are taken with very important people. It very often works, because most congressmen have egos large enough to qualify for work in grand opera. There is the party loyalty appeal—our great leader needs you. There are innumerable other appeals. And there is sex appeal, including photographs which can be made available to wronged congressional wives. Indeed, a Capitol Hill wag tells me that according to current word, the Capitol dome is lit only when a congressman is busy with his girl friend, and it is of course lit every night.

Several years ago former Senator William B. Spong, Democrat of Virginia, used his own and the names of his colleagues, for a little sound-effects play at a banquet of the Women's National Press Club (now the Washington Press Club).

Forgoing poetry for the moment, it was suggested I might discuss a new legislative objective, namely, to strengthen international agreements in order to stop the piracy of American music by publishers in Hong Kong. With the Senator from Hawaii who is closer to the situation, and the Senator from Louisiana, the home of American Jazz, I hope to co-sponsor what well may come to be known as the "Long-Fong-Spong Hong Kong Song Bill."

* * *

And Republican Representatives James R. Grover of New York and James C. Cleveland of New Hampshire decided the historical accident of their combined surnames might be good reason for a law declaring a new holiday.

A DEPLORABLE HOLIDAY SITUATION

Following last year's landmark legislation making certain holidays fall on Mondays, and the addition of Columbus Day as a holiday, there has been some interest in adding deserving dates as national holidays.

However meritorious the many recent proposals are, a most meaningful one has gone unrecognized—March 18, which is Grover Cleveland's birthday. This suggestion is offered in the most bipartisan of spirits, as we are both Republicans, and this renowned President was a Democrat.

In keeping with recent policy, our proposal is to observe this holiday on the fourth Monday in March, so as to give America an additional three-day weekend. A significant advantage of this proposal is that now we go from February to May without a legal holiday. Our bill would remedy this deplorable situation.

If you wish to be a co-sponsor of this significant legislation, please call either of our offices before March 22.

Signed: *James R. Grover, Jr., Member of Congress*
James G. Cleveland, Member of Congress

* * *

The wit of Minority Leader Senator Hugh Scott of Pennsylvania and the leisurely anecdotes of Democratic Senator Sam Ervin of North Carolina surface on almost any subject. In June, 1972, in the Senate chamber, Scott expressed this random thought on the weather:

THE UNJUST HAVE JUST THE UMBRELLA

Mr. President, this is the day that the Lord hath made, and I hope that we will all, therefore, make the best use of it.

I have a random thought that it is fortunate for the people of this country that the weather is the product of natural forces or sublime direction, rather than the work of a committee or of Congress, because I am sure that if the weather were up to Congress, this body would be engaged in arguments over whether we should have clear or partly cloudy weather. The other body would then opt for showers—especially the Committee on Agriculture and Forestry, or the committee interested in irrigation, livestock, and so forth. And then, from time to time, over here we would have one of those familiar reversals where someone would filibuster in order to get rain on this side of the Capitol as well. Then there would be a spate of press releases to the public claiming credit for the rain which had fallen on the just and unjust alike.

Then the populace would be claiming that while the rain falls alike upon the just and the unjust fellow, it falls more often on that just because the unjust have just the umbrella.

*   *   *

In March of 1971, Scott said the old Know Nothingism was based on illiteracy and groundless fear. The new Know Nothingism is based on literacy and groundless fear.

*   *   *

Senator Sam Ervin had this comparison to make between the Bible and the *Congressional Record:*

I believe it will be rather interesting to senators to compare the thickness of this large pile of Congressional Records *with the thickness of the Good Book which contains the words of the Lord. This large pile of* Congressional Records *is nine and a half inches thick. I am certainly glad that when the Good Lord saw fit to give us the Book which would tell us all we need to know about our sins on this earth and about how we can get to heaven, he was not as verbose as the members of the United States Senate were between February 24 and April 9, 1960, because if the Good Lord had been that verbose, we would never be able to read the Bible, even if we devoted all our time to it between the cradle and the grave.*

REPLACE POLITICIANS WITH COMPUTERS

Ervin also said the day may come when we will replace politicians with computers.

Judging from some of the reasoning of politicians I've seen over the years, I know I would sooner take the logic of a computer. The machine may suffer the same lack of intelligence as some politicians, but at least there is consistency in its idiocy.

*   *   *

The North Carolina Senator also tells this one:

Those in public life are sometimes subject to the same experience as that of the young man who was persuaded to become a candidate for the state legislature. His father tried to persuade him not to go into politics. He said, "Son, don't go into politics. If you get into this race for the legislature, before it's over they will accuse you of stealing a horse."

The son did not take his father's advice. He plunged into the race. After the election was over he came back home defeated. His father said, "Son, didn't I say to you that you would be accused of stealing a horse before the election was over?"

And the son replied, "Pa, it's much worse that that. They darn near proved it on me."

RIVER JORDAN ON CONNALLY RANCH

At the Washington Press Club dinner in January of 1973, Democratic Representative Barbara Jordan of Texas, one of the new members of Congress invited to speak, was asked this question, "Tell us, what happened when John Connally and his People reached the Jordan?" The freshman Black congresswoman replied:

They stopped. The water was black you know and somewhat treacherous. John pondered whether it would be safer to cross party lines than to cross the Jordan.

John Connally considered the river. He asked a henchman how much it would cost to divert that little old stream to his ranch near San Antonio. But, then, who wants a river named Jordan on a Connally Ranch?

A new idea flashed through his mind, his first new thought since the new economic policy. We'll change the name of the blasted stream. We'll call it Big John. Big John? BJ? Not on your life!! Illiterate Texans would think it stood for Barbara Jordan.

A second idea fought its way to his awareness. "We'll buy the river and set up a Holy water franchise." We'll bottle it for the Episcopalians and sell it by the tank to the Baptists.

The only problem with this is the name of the blasted stream.

He finally said, "What the hell, let's grab a limousine and go back to the Hilton. A camel driver will show us the way."

Guess what was the name of the hotel? . . . the Jordan Hilton.

And before the Idaho Wildlife Federation on March 18, 1972, another Jordan in the Congress, Republican Senator Len B. of Idaho, began his speech with this anecdote:

Arriving back in the state in the midst of a pre-primary election campaign reminds me of my first statewide venture into elective politics.

I was one of five entries in a race for nomination as a candidate for the Governorship, and one of the least known statewide. On one of my first forays into the state to get my name known, I was engaged in hand-shaking in a small community and was pleasantly surprised to run into a man who told me I was his second choice for the Governorship.

A Blow Below the Political Belt

I thanked him for his confidence in me and then, as if to prove that I was no politician, I asked him who his first choice was.

"Oh, just about any one of the other four candidates," he replied.

* * *

And part of this dialogue on the floor of the Senate to get the Congress recessed and off on its Easter interlude is a splendid verbal minuet involving Democratic Majority Leaker Mike Mansfield of Montana and Wyoming's Democratic Senator Gale McGee.

Mr. McGee: . . . I was wondering whether it might be more practicable to develop the scheduling of the opening dialogue of this measure on the return of senators. I hasten to add that the Senator from Wyoming is going to be here the entire week, and he would just as soon we discussed it on Friday or Saturday next.

Mr. Mansfield: No. Good Friday is a day we all like to observe. Holy Saturday is a day we all like to observe. Easter is a day we all like to commemorate, because of what lies behind it.

We will have plenty of time on this bill. I would not want to come back after meeting later this afternoon and get started. I think it would be very sparse. Tomorrow will be a good day, at about 11 o'clock.

Mr. McGee: *The Senator from Wyoming is ready to proceed either right now or to defer to the commitments of his colleagues and proceed tomorrow at 11 o'clock. Is that the time we will meet tomorrow?*

Mr. Mansfield: *Yes.*

Mr. McGee: *And await his turn in line for the dropping of pearls of wisdom that the circumstances will permit.*

Mr. Mansfield: *May I say that the Senator from Wyoming, for some reason, reminds me of a colt scratching the ground, waiting to get out the gate or corral to get going. I am sure we will have plenty of time.*

Mr. McGee: *Well, the Derby is not very far off. It is spring, and there are colts that are very impatient, even though the Senator from Wyoming is confined to a Mustang with its top down. So we will begin the dialogue tomorrow morning at about 11?*

Mr. Mansfield: *After the morning business.*

*   *   *

When Democratic Senator Carl Hayden of Arizona retired, Senator Eugene McCarthy noted that the Senate is the last primitive society in the world. "We still worship the elders of the tribe and honor the territorial imperative," he said. "We are now struggling to see who gets Senator Hayden's cave."

In 1967 in Pennsylvania Senator McCarthy said:

We say around the Senate that you can get a reading about how weak a man's position is by what he quotes. If he starts out with the Bible, you know he is in pretty bad trouble. Then if he tries to defend his position with the Constitution, you know he is in worse trouble. Finally, if he appeals to the rules of the Senate, you know he is in real trouble. That is a last point of appeal. . . .

In the Senate they insist every year, when the rules are up for revision, that the Senate is a continuing body. They are a little vague about when it started, but they are sure it will never have an ending. The accepted view seems to be that as long as some senator is either speaking or is free to speak, the Republic will not fall. It is a kind of democratic version of the Vestal Virgins that we have developed here in the United States.

SENATOR EVERETT DIRKSEN: A petunia, my dear dog Dum-Dum, is very different from a marigold.

CHAPTER FIFTEEN

The Senate Gets Spring Fever

ALMOST NO FLOWERS WERE BLOOMING

Exchanges on the floor of the Senate and House spark some of the more subtle, leisurely congressional humor—the kind indulged in around a stove in the general store of the country's beginnings. One of the perennials during any spring season for many years has been a break out of flowers on the Senate floor. Here is one which took place in April a few years back:

Mr. Humphrey: *I noted with surprise that in this city, where spring comes early, almost no flowers were blooming anywhere in the immediate vicinity of the Capitol building.*

The calendar tells us that spring has come. If we step outside right now, we can feel that it is spring. The flowers which are blooming in the private yards and gardens throughout the Washington area tell us it is spring. The gardens surrounding the center of the executive branch of our government—the White House—tell us it is spring. Even the leaves and the trees surrounding the Capitol tell us rather plaintively that it is spring.

But there are no flowers in the eastern area of the Capitol grounds to tell us that it is spring. The beautiful fountain in front of the Capitol is dry; there is no water.

I should like to see improved gardens and far more blossoms surrounding the Capitol. I think the thousands of American citizens who visit the nation's capital, would like to see more flowers around the Capitol.

The government operates hundreds of plant research laboratories and sustains thousands of specialists who work in the field of horticulture and agronomy. It would seem proper for us to expend just a little effort to make certain that the Capitol—itself a beautiful structure—is fringed with gardens and with the color of flowers.

Possibly I am taking this all too seriously, but it appears to me that there needs to be some note of beauty in our deliberations; and the purpose of my remarks is to nudge my colleagues out of their deep, somber concern for earth-shaking budgets and policy deliberations for a few moments to consider a small—but important—need in the front yard of the nation's government.

No Relaxation for the Feet

Washington is a beautiful city, primarily because of its wide boulevards and white, gleaming buildings. Let us add to it the beauty of providing the natural colors and blossoms of nature. I, for one, will appreciate it. So will the millions of citizens who journey to the Capitol city each year.

This brings me to a second brief thought. The visitors to the Capitol do not find adequate facilities on these grounds to relax their feet for a moment and enjoy the views from Capitol Hill. Only a few benches are scattered around the terraces and grounds of the Capitol. More are needed. I ask any senator to accompany his own constituents around the Capitol grounds. What he will recognize during his tour will be the great need for such facilities. Not a bench will be found; not a table will be found. No opportunity is afforded for lunch or refreshment; not even a cold water fountain for a cool drink of clean water. I suggest that the least that can be done is to provide such facilities. . . .

The Gentle Multicolored Pansies

Mr. Dirksen: Mr. President, I am always transported by the profound observations made by my distinguished friend, the senior Senator from Minnesota [Mr. Humphrey]; but never am I quite so transported as when he ventures into the domain of flowers.

Today he has made an eloquent entreaty to have the Capitol grounds fairly bedecked with nature's choicest flowers, to delight the eyes and the hearts of the thousands of Americans who come here.

I share the great interest of the Senator from Minnesota in this matter, but it does involve somewhat of a problem. You see, Mr. President, insofar as I recall, the average date of the last frost in the Washington area is April 20; but the gardeners usually figure that there may be a frost as late as the first of May.

Of course, there are frost-resistent flowers. For instance, let us consider the gentle, multicolored pansies. They can be planted in the winter; and when spring comes, after the winter has ended, we find them with their beautiful dainty heads, helping to beautify the world.

Then there is the daffodil, a hardy flower. I remember the little ode by Wordsworth:

"Ten thousand saw I at a glance,
Tossing their heads in sprightly dance."

But we cannot cover the entire Capitol grounds with daffodils.

The gardeners have always graced the Capitol grounds with cannas, but of course they are not very frost resistant. So the gardeners do the proper thing, and the cannas are planted later in the season.

The dahlias always entrance the eye; but one must be careful lest the tiny shoots of the dahlias come up before the frosts end, in which case it is necessary to do the work all over again.

Then there is the gentle petunia, one of my favorite flowers. But one must be careful about when he plants them.

Certainly I wish to see the Capitol grounds bedecked and beautiful, Mr. President; but I am afraid that my distinguished friend, the Senator from Minnesota, has failed to read the old almanac, which tells us that in April frost may occur at any time; and, of course, if frost comes, it is necessary to do the planting of flowers all over again.

Nature's Own Sweet Time

Thus it is, Mr. President, that the Senator from Minnesota and I and the toursits must wait for nature, and must permit nature to take its own sweet time. We must take into account the seasons and the time when the frosts end.

Of course, I am an amateur; and I planted my cannas this weekend, in the hope that there will be no more frost this season.

Certainly in due time there will be cannas and dahlias and princess feathers and, in due time, all the other beautiful flowers, that somehow engender a kind of introspection, assuage all the turbulence of the soul, and bring peace to the hearts of all those who labor here and of all the thousands who come here to visit. So, Mr. President, all in its own good time will be brought to pass.

Mr. Humphrey: *Mr. President, will the Senator from Illinois yield?*

Mr. Dirksen: *I yield.*

Mr. Humphrey: *I am happy that the distinguished Minority Leader, the Senator from Illinois, has given us this note of reassurance, because my heart was troubled and my spirit was dampened by the knowledge that many of these flowers are not planted on the Capitol grounds. However, the reassurance we have received from the Minority Leader gives me a ray of hope, and I think I can hang on for a few days more.*

But I should like to say that although undoubtedly the Senator from Illinois is an expert on horticulture, he is much less expert when he deals with matters of temperature. I would be delighted to have the Senator stop by the neighborhood where I live in Maryland. It is far enough away from the Capitol so that the air out there is not quite as warm as it is here. I would like to have him see the beautiful flowers of some of my neighbors. It is a little more frosty in the country than it is in this urban area.

The New Frontier Draws the Frost Line?

There are also beautiful flowers at the White House. I did not know the power of the New Frontier was so great that it could draw the frost line where it wanted to, even though it might be helpful. . . .

Mr. Dirksen: *Now, Mr. President . . .*

Mr. Humphrey: *I merely want to say to the Senator that he has been very reassuring. It was my hope that this colloquy would permit some further improvement of the grounds. I know now that I have strong, staunch support in this famous soldier of agronomy from Illinois.*

Mr. Dirksen: *In my observations I should have mentioned the stately tulip, but I am afraid my friend is making reference to shrubs.*

Mr. Humphrey: *No. The Senator from Minnesota knows the difference between a shrub and a flower.*

Mr. Dirksen: *Shrubs such as forsythia and dogwood and other plants are presently coming into bloom. But I remind my friend that "Weeping may endure for a night, but joy cometh in the morning."*

Be reassured.

Mr. Humphrey: *I join with the distinguished Senator and offer him my hand in the interest of horticulture and better shrubs and flowers.*

Dirksen's Flowery Language

The next day the exchange continued:

Mr. Humphrey: *Mr. President, I am delighted to see the affable, the* loquacious, and the distinguished and able minority leader, the Senator from Illinois (Mr. Dirksen), in the Chamber, because as of yesterday he gave me a graduate course in horticulture, flower raising, varieties of flowers in flowery language that did something for my soul. It was senatorial poetry.

I wish to compliment Mr. John Lindsay on his article published in the Washington Post this morning for relating to the readers of the Washington Post what had transpired in the Senate. If nothing else had happened yesterday, this alone was worthwhile. At least a certain amount of column space was taken up on a subject matter that has some spiritual and esthetic content; namely, the beauty of the Washington area, and the potentiality of beautifying this area even beyond what it is at present.

However, I take exception with one or two points in the article. I am pleased to note that the Minority Leader is on the floor. He can help us, and give us further education in these matters, particularly now that it is the beginning of spring.

Since yesterday, I have been doing some research on the subject of flowers, blooms, shrubs, trees, and plants.

While the distinguished Senator from Illihois was quite flowery in his language, and while his dissertation flowed like a brook following the spring rains, I thought that its objectivity was not quite equal to its aesthetic quality.

The Senator from Illinois, I am sure, would enjoy visiting the National Arboretum in Washington. I have come prepared today with information that will be of help to my colleagues in case they wish to explore this matter in more detail. I have before me the U.S. Department of Agriculture pamphlet on the National Arboretum. It is Pamphlet No. 309.

I call the attention of the Senator from Illinois to the fact that the Arboretum is administered by the Department of Agriculture through the Crops Research Division of the Agricultural Research Service. It was established by act of Congress on March 4, 1927, and is located in the northeast section of the District of Columbia at M Street and Maryland Avenue. I thought I would give that as a guideline so that senators who may be interested in visiting the Arboretum will not end up out at the stadium or armory.

Only Five Minutes More?

The Acting President pro tempore: The time of the Senator has expired.

Mr. Humphrey: *I ask for five additional minutes.*

The Acting President pro tempore: *Is there objection? The Chair hears none, and the Senator may proceed.*

Mr. Humphrey: *The purpose of the Arboretum is to conduct research with woody plants and shrubs susceptible of cultivation in the climate prevailing in the Washington area.*

Here is what the senators would see. For example, there is the rhododendron, with its handsome white, pink, or rose-purple flowers. The Cornell pink variety of the rhododendron was developed by the director of the National Arboretum, Dr. H. T. Skinner, when he was at Cornell. It blooms from late March to early April. I believe there are about twenty varieties of the rhododendron that grow in the Washington area, with beautiful coloration. We could have had these in bloom around the Capitol. All these beautiful blooms could have been here for us to admire despite the professional knowledge of the amateur gardener from Illinois.

Then there is the Camellia Japonica, which was derived and introduced by a Jesuit priest, Father Kamel, early in the seventeenth century. It has glossy evergreen leaves and red or white double roselike flowers and blooms from mid-March to mid-April. We could have had a whole month of these beautiful blooms and flowers to admire, despite the dissertation of the Senator from Illinois expressing worry about frost and whether or not these flowers would grow at this time of year.

Andromeda Was an Ethiopian Princess

Then there is the Callery pear tree of Pyrus calleryiana. A new variety of it, released in 1960, is now available. This blooms from early April to mid-April. We have lost the opportunity to enjoy these beautiful blooms because of misinformation such as that expressed by the Senator from Illinois.

Then there is the Pieris Japonica, or Andromeda, with its lily-of-the-valley-type bloom. Andromeda, the senators will recall, was an Ethiopian princess who was chained to a cliff for a monster to devour, but was rescued by Perseus, who married her. This blooms from late March to late April. It blooms right here in Washington. We have lost a whole month because of the gardening habits or horticultural knowledge of the distinguished and able Senator From Illinois, which was erroneous.

Mr. Douglas of Illinois: *Mr. President, will the Senator yield?*

Mr. Humphrey: *I yield.*

Mr. Douglas: *I do not wish to make this an Illinois-Minnesota collo-quy, but in as much as the Senator from Minnesota has mentioned the sad fate of Andromeda, I should like to inquire whether he is going to play the part of Perseus and rescue Andromeda from her chained position on the rock?*

Mr. Humphrey: *That sounds like an honorable and chivalrous activity. I would not mind having the privilege of doing that.*

Then, of course, there are varieties of flowers that bloom from early April, up to early May, in this climate. They are the pansy, the daffodil, and the tulip. I want to compliment the distinguished Senator from Illinois for mentioning the daffodil. He spoke about how beautiful is the daffodil. Then, why do we not have daffodils planted around the Capitol? He also spoke of the tulip. All over Washington one sees tulips in bloom at this time of year. We could have had many tulips blooming around the Capitol, and thus honor one of our NATO allies, Holland, at the same time.

The Potentials of the Crocus

The Acting President pro tempore: *The time of the Senator has expired.*

Mr. Humphrey: *I must continue. I ask for additional time. It is hard to discuss a subject like this in five minutes.*

The Acting President pro tempore: *Is there objection? The Chair hears none, and the Senator may proceed.*

Mr. Case of South Dakota: *Mr. President, will the Senator yield?*

Mr. Humphrey: *I yield.*

Mr. Case of South Dakota: *I trust that the distinguished Senator from Minnesota, who is presently displaying this wide knowledge of flowers, will not forget the state of his birth, South Dakota, and overlook the potentials of the crocus.*

Mr. Humphrey: *I was coming to that, I assure the Senator.*

Mr. Case of South Dakota: *The Anemone is the state flower of South Dakota.*

Mr. Humphrey: *My heart was opening like a tulip or crocus.*

Mr. Aiken of Vermont: *It seems to me that the Anemone—sometimes called pasque flower—and the crocus should not be confused. There is a European species called anemone pulsatilla. The anemone patens is the state flower of South Dakota.*

Mr. Humphrey: *There is an apparent fund of knowledge about flowers in the Senate, including the Latin names of many of them.*

Mr. Aiken: *The state flower of South Dakota is not a crocus.*

Mr. Humphrey: *We call it the crocus.*

Mr. Aiken: *The Anemone patens is the state flower of South Dakota. It is an anemone. . . .*

Mr. Case of South Dakota: *Yes. The anemone is the name of the flower that we apply to the publication of the Black Hills Teachers College at Spearfish. "Pasque Petals" is the name of the South Dakota poetry magazine. However, I will say that most of us in the spring go out looking for the crocus.*

From the Blood of Hyacinthus

Mr. Humphrey: *The Senator is correct. Then there is the hyacinth, a plant fabled in the classic mythology to have sprung from the blood of Hyacinthus, a youth beloved by Apollo and accidently killed by him. From his blood Apollo caused the hyacinth to spring.*

Here again is a flower that blooms in Washington, and one we could have enjoyed during the past month. It is derived from one of the great stories of mythology. We could have had our citizenry think about all this, had these flowers been planted around the terrace of the Capitol.

Then there is the crocus, which will come up through the snow, and the forsythia, a plant with yellow bell-shaped flowers, appearing before the leaves in the early spring.

All these blooms and flowers would have blossomed even before April.

Among the woody plants, there is the dogwood and the redbud, with its heart-shaped leaves and small pink flowers. Both blossom from late April to early May.

Then, of course, there is the azalea, which starts blooming in late April and continues through May. Right now there are beautiful azaleas in bloom at the National Arboretum. There are literally dozens of varieties of azaleas. All these may be seen at the National Arboretum. . . .

Sometime, when the Senator from Illinois is traveling to and from work, he should drive by the Department of the Interior, where a small park faces Virginia Avenue. In it he will see beautiful pansy beds. Pansies have been blooming there for the last three weeks. They have been blooming, that is, in front of the Department of the Interior, not at the Capitol, where thousands of our fellow citizens come every day to visit.

Or the Senator might drive by the Tidal Basin and see the beautiful azaleas and hyacinths which have been in bloom for three weeks.

Flowers Everywhere at Flower Show

Mr. President, I wish to pay tribute to the many flower clubs throughout the United States. Everyone should go to a flower show and see the beautiful early varieties. A flower show was held in Washington during the first part of March. It was a sight to behold. Flowers were everywhere, and all of them beautiful. Flower clubs have made a notable contribution to the development of new varieties. They should be commended and encouraged to continue to expand their fine efforts.

Now as to frosts. I now realize why we have had such a bad winter — storms and floods. It is because for several years the Weather Bureau has been under Republican jurisdiction. After listening to the distinguished Minority Leader yesterday, I can plainly understand why we cannot rely on Republican weather forecasts. According to the actual statistics, the last frost in 1961 — that is, with the temperature at 32 degrees — was on April 3. The average date of the last frost in Washington is April 10.

Mind you, Mr. President, all the flowers of which we have spoken thus far seem to endure frost with little or no trouble.

They are hardy plants, particularly the crocus, the tulip, the hyacinth, and the rhododendron; and all of them are beautiful plants.

The Senator from Illinois [Mr. Dirksen] was, however, accurate in one detail. The latest date of a frost this year 1962 was April 20 — that is, for the suburbs. But we are now talking about the Capital. The latest date on record for a frost in Washington is May 12, 1913. That is, according to the records of the Weather Bureau.

So, Mr. President, I thought perhaps we ought to set the record straight. I know that I am about to receive another one of the Senator's eloquent responses.

The Presiding Officer [Mr. Jordan in the chair]: *The time of the Senator from Minnesota has expired.*

Mr. Humphrey: *Mr. President, I ask for an additional minute.*

The Presiding Officer: *Without objection, it is so ordered.*

Mr. Humphrey: *Mr. President, Mr. Lindsay of the Post said: "The next time Senator Hubert Humphrey has a complaint about the paucity of flowers blooming at the Capitol, he'll probably keep it to himself."*

I suppose a wise and prudent man would have done that, but I am more reckless. Mr. Lindsay continued:

Verbal Petals from Senator Dirksen

"The scarcity of blooms was all he had in mind yesterday when he took the Senate floor. But somehow he pulled the lever and went down under a gentle torrent of verbal petals that fell from the lips of Senator Everett Dirksen."

I would say that was terrific. I am deeply indebted to our good friend from Illinois. But I thought that since he had inspired me to so great a love of nature, I would do some research. So I studied the National Gardener, the Fern Valley Trail, and a History of the National Arboretum, and other publications.

I have learned that camellias, tulips, pansies, hyacinths, are recommended for the Washington area, as are rhododendron and azaleas, all of which the distinguished Senator from Illinois should know, but first it is necessary to plant them.

Also I have acquired a "hardiness weather zone map." I suggest the Minority Leader study it. This is no trouble for the distinguished Senator. His knowledge of the weather, varieties of plants and flowers, of soil and topographical conditions is of little help to his knowledge of the terraces of the Capitol in Washington, D.C. He is an expert on Illinois planting conditions, but when it comes to Washington, D.C., he is a fiction writer. But his voice does flow like the gentle breeze when he talks about the beautiful flowers.

After the Senator from Illinois has given me another lecture about flowers, I hope he will try to assist me in securing a few benches to be placed on the Mall and around the Capitol terraces, so that visitors will be able to take a rest. I know the Senator from Illinois knows how to build benches, too; so I am prepared to take my seat for the next lecture.

Mr. Dirksen: Mr. President, the Senator from Minnesota not only pulled the wrong lever yesterday, but he has been pulling it all day and all night, assembling all these data. He reminds me of an agricultural specialist who went to South Dakota and visited a farm. Finally he got his ire up and said to the farmer, "I don't believe you could get any more than two quarts of milk out of that goat." The farmer said, "You are so right. It isn't a goat; it's a sheep."

A Shrub Is a Shrub Is a Shrub

Yesterday the Senator was talking about flowers. Today he talks about forsythia. Well, I suppose anyone who has had anything to do with flowers knows that forsythia is a shrub. The Senator from Minnesota has spoken of azaleas. With rare success, I have tried to coax them out of the acid soil. But the azalea is a shrub, not a flower.

The Senator speaks in glowing terms about the delicate shades of rhododendron. How wonderfully right he is, except that the rhododendron is a shrub which grows quite high. It is not a flower at all.

When it comes to the narcissus, of course, it is possible to grow narcissus which are frostproof. However, they do not last very long.

The gardeners who look after the Capitol, when they fill the empty beds, seek to plant flowers that will stand up and bloom all through the late spring and summer to delight the eyes of the thousands of visitors to the Capitol.

So, Mr. President, I am going to take my friend in hand.

Mr. Humphrey: *Ah, good.*

Mr. Dirksen: *I am going to take him out to those rather impoverished acres of mine and give him some elementary lectures on the difference between a flower and a shrub.*

Mr. Humphrey: *Mr. President, I know the Senator from Illinois would want to yield. I have seen shrubs with their blooms on occasion, even in the acid soil; and when the blooms are forthcoming, we call them flowers—that is, we simple country folk call them flowers. I cannot say what the professional person calls them. But if the Senator from Illinois does not think the beautiful azalea is a flower, he should talk to the ladies about them, because they consider them lovely blooms, lovely flowers, just as they consider the blooms of the rhododendron and other shrubs, flowers, and blossoms of beauty and grace.*

But I take the Senator's word. His flowery language overwhelms me, and makes me feel he knows more about flowers than I will ever know. I will accept the statement of the senatorial professor of horticulture.

Mr. Dirksen: *Whenever the Senator from Minnesota can convert the Senate or anyone else who is rooted in the soil to believe that a flower is a shrub, I will nominate him to the next vacant seat on the Supreme Court of the United States.*

Mr. Humphrey: *I thank the Senator from Illinois.*

CHAPTER SIXTEEN

Laughs Hang on the Congressman's Family Tree

NOW THAT HIS NAUSEA HAS SUBSIDED

In the annals of American humor a famous or purportedly odd-ball relative has always been a great springboard for a yarn. Congressional humor is right in there with contributions.

Senator James Buckley, Republican of New York, uses this exchange of letters between himself and his brother, author William Buckley, to thaw out audiences. He says he received this letter from a constituent:

Hon.? James Buckley, Senate Office Building, Washington, D.C.

Sir: Now that my nausea has subsided after accidentally observing your appearance on "Laugh-In" last evening I, as one of your constituents and former admirers, am constrained to comment.

Your silly grin as the inane and vulgar questions were asked and your equally inane replies were less than worthy of a Senator of the United States.

The fact that you appeared on the program at all was an insult to the decent people whom you represent.

The disgusting episode in which you freely participated and apparently enjoyed—as an accomplice in lending your position to a disgraceful program—is an affront to the dignity of the Senate, to your family, to your church, and to your constituency. I trust that your acting the clown insured the support of the addicts of the program who undoubtedly enjoy its indecencies. I trust, too, that they are in the minority. I am. . . .

SA ZSA GABOR TO PENNSYLVANIA SENATOR HUGH SCOTT (left) AND NEW YORK
ENATOR JAMES BUCKLEY: Darlings!   Senate Photo by Jules Schick

April 1, 1971

Sir:

I have forwarded your letter to my Brother the Columnist—William F. Buckley, Jr.

It was he, not I, who appeared on "Laugh-In."

I can't help but be curious as to why you consented to watch a program of which you so strongly disapprove.

Sincerely, [signed] James L. Buckley.

Happily, Bill was able to put my constituent's mind at ease with the following letter:

Dear Sir: It is typical of my brother to attempt to deceive his constituents. It was, of course, he, not I, who appeared on "Laugh-In." Just as you suspected. On the other hand, you need not worry about it. His greatest deception is as yet undiscovered. It was I, not he, who was elected to the Senate. So you see, you have nothing to worry about. You are represented in the Senate by a responsible, truthful man.

Yours, William F. Buckley, Jr.

NUTTISM, SKIN-GAME-ISM, AND SNAKE-CHUNKING

And Senator Russell Long, Democrat of Louisiana, has built into his family humorous springboards for almost anything he wants to say. His late father, Huey Long, United States Senator and Governor of Louisiana, and his late Uncle Earl, Governor of Louisiana, were two of the most colorful politicians who ever turned up in southern United States or any other part of the nation. And a lot of their color was in their relating what happened to them in their political and legislative lives.

Sometimes Senator Long illustrates with this one, how a politician may achieve a legislative end in more ways than one:

When a new hospital for the underprivileged was built in Louisiana, Negro politicians complained to Governor Huey Long that there were no Negro nurses working there, even though half the patients were Negro. The governor told them he would fix it, but they wouldn't like the way he did it. He made a big fuss in the media about white nurses being humiliated and lowered by taking care of colored men. Racist talk it was indeed, but a lot of colored nurses got jobs in the hospital, and have had them ever since.

Senator Long also tells about his Uncle Earl not being against any ism except nuttism, skin-game-ism or communism, and being in favor of every religion with the possible exception of snake-chunking. He always adds that followers of this sect, who would let a snake bite them, do not vote.

*   *   *

The Louisiana Democrat also tells this story which his Uncle Earl used when he wanted to take a jab at rich folks:

It seems St. Peter couldn't find much reason for a certain rich man getting into Heaven. So at the Golden Gate the rich man started telling St. Peter about times when he had been charitable. He said on a cold day a few years after the turn of the century he had given a blind man a nickel. The records were checked and there was the entry, but St. Peter didn't feel that was enough to make up for his otherwise selfish life. But the rich man persisted, while the Devil waited in the wings to take him below. He told about the time in the twenties when he gave a poor widow lady.five cents for carfare. Among all his recorded bad deeds, this also was found. St. Peter didn't think that was enough either. The Devil began to move in. But the rich man insisted, and told about the nickel he gave to the Red Cross during the depression.

To which St. Peter replied, "Give him back his fifteen cents and tell him to go to Hell."

JOHN TUNNEY AND CASSIUS CLAY IN THREE ROUNDS

At the January, 1971 annual congressional dinner of the Washington Press Club Democratic Senator Adlai Stevenson III of Illinois had this to say:

. . . I was told tonight that I had to equal my father's wit and eloquence for two and a half minutes. I accepted the challenge—but only with the understanding that after I've had the chance to match my father's skills you will call upon John Tunney to come forward and take Cassius Mohammad Ali Clay on for three rounds.

I do want to report on my first two months in the Senate. My rise has been meteoric. I entered ranking 100th among the 100 senators in seniority. And now I rank 89th. I've even been assigned to the District Committee.

But humility comes easily in the Senate. The day I was sworn in we found two thousand letters that were waiting for me, and the first I saw was from a voter back home who asked me where I thought I'd be if my name were Harry Stevenson, Herman Stevenson, or even Robert Louis Stevenson. Then one sent me a postcard suggesting that "If anyone says you are not a red blooded patriot, hit him with your purse."

I have nonetheless decided tonight to give a little friendly advice to the junior senators present.

My first advice is don't ever get rattled. In language befitting your juniority, keep your cool.

I was sworn in a day ahead of schedule on thirty minutes' notice because the leadership thought my vote might be needed on a pending roll call. Minutes after taking the oath I listened intently as the clerk called the roll—Aiken, Allen, Allot. The names grew closer. Sparkman, "No," Stennis, "No," Stevens—and I said "Aye."

It was Stevens of Alaska. But I didn't get rattled. The clerk called Stevenson—and I said "Aye" again.

Two Votes for a Cook County Boy

And so it was that on my first roll call in the United States Senate I voted twice—not a bad start for a Cook County boy.

Next—don't let the name plate on your office door lull you into a false sense of seniority.

An hour after I was sworn in I took possession of a suite on the first floor of the OSOB—historic and commodious quarters occupied in bygone years by some of the most illustrious figures in the history of the Senate.

A few days after we had put up our welcome sign, we started receiving visits from small delegations of senior senators and staff whose solicitude was most gratifying. They wanted to be sure I found the location of my office convenient to the Senate subway and the gymnasium, that the offices were not drafty and so on. I assumed they were all part of some senatorial welcome wagon.

I know better now. They were spies. They coveted my high ceilings and fireplaces, the alcoves, my six spacious offices.

So I am about to be evicted. But tomorrow morning I intend to take a hard look at Hubert Humphrey's quarters.

I am aware that you have a ruthless cloture rule. I'm grateful to you for inviting me. This is the first time since 1893 that a funny thing hasn't *happened to a Stevenson on his way to Washington. I'm very glad to be here.*

BETWEEN A PILGRIM AND A RAKE

Representative James W. Symington, Democrat of Missouri, who sings, plays the guitar, and has served as Chief of Protocol in the Department of State, is the son of Senator Stuart Symington, Democrat of Missouri. He also spoke at a Washington Press Club Dinner:

The question as I see it is—
Was it protocol, Dad, or the old guitar that brought me along to where I are.
I have had little time to polish my verse serving as I do in the House.
But I'd like to trace briefly my progress which some say has been more or less between that of a pilgrim and a rake—so you can judge for yourselves. At the time of my appointment to Protocol I had been fighting juvenile delinquency, almost single handed. Having pretty well eliminated it, the transition to protocol seemed normal enough. Still, it required some new disciplines. My wife and friends for example pointed out I might have to modify the little habit I had of smacking the palms of my hands on the table, kicking my feet out, and shouting "din din" as meals were served. With this somewhat stricter personal code I entered the State Department, affectionately dubbed by White House intellectuals as the "Fink Tank." I was determined to learn from the mistakes of my predecessors; unfortunately they didn't make any so I had to learn from my own. Luckily I made a great many so I learned a lot. My performances in the delicate tasks assigned to me often brought the President to his feet, or at least one of them. But as the President once kindly said, "Jim, anyone can make mistakes, but in Protocol you've made mistakes for your country!"

Ambassadors Escorted into Cul-de-Sacs

During my term of office, ambassadors were escorted into cul-de-sacs, former invitations to Heads of State were abruptly cancelled, embassies were bombed, diplomats assaulted and robbed, butlers shot, relations with seven nations severed, and after devaluation of the pound, the British flag flown upside down by the Honor Guard while the Prime

Minister was treated to a White House serenade of "I've got plenty of nuthin."

I think it may have been this unbroken and touching display of virtuosity that moved the President one day last year to ask if I had ever thought of running for Congress. Even as he spoke, Marvin Watson was removing my cummerbund, my patent leather pumps, my fall. I was actually debriefed in the Fish Room. Then, delicately, I left the White House, and went to the nearest phone booth to tell my father the good news.

"Dad," I said, "guess what, I'm running, no, not jogging. Congress. From where?! From Missouri. Will you support me, Pop? I know you've been supporting me a long time—just this little kicker. Well, would you stay neutral? Gee, thanks, Dad, you know you're a real senior senator to me."

Thus reassured, I plunged into politics, and took firm positions from the start. Regardless of Mayor Daley's reasoned approach I felt a lutist should not be shot, especially if playing his own lute. Warned, cursed, pushed, and kicked, of course, but not otherwise harmed.

Roll Eggheads on the White House Lawn

Over the heads of seething crowds, I proclaimed my slogan: "Register Democrats, not guitars!" And, oh, how the crowd roared back . . . if only they had agreed!

Still, many times I was carried away in triumph on their shoulders—bound and gagged.

So we face a new day—new ideas—changes—like the Easter plan to roll eggheads on the White House lawn. We must live with change—at least until under some future administration we can have dollars again.

In the meantime, to all the folks out there in radioland I know what you want of me is to remain alert and attentive to the opportunities presented in the 91st Congress, and I can hardly wait until it convenes to prove your confidence is not misplaced.

CHAPTER SEVENTEEN

Congress on Stage

THE KENNEDYS COULDN'T PLAY LEADS

When members of Congress have been in the theatrical business, their earlier experience makes a good springboard for the politics of humor.

Representative Dan Flood begins many a speech by saying he is a congressman today because he was once a leading man.

"Then some casting director told me a leading man deteriorated with age," the Pennsylvania Democrat says. "The fellow suggested I had better begin in a few years thinking about character parts I could play."

Flood says he was young then, and the idea of playing a park-bench bum, a disintegrating owner of a Mississippi Show Boat, or an aging rancher didn't send him. So he went instead to law school, entered politics, and came to Washington to play a role he knew he could relish and enjoy for a long time, that of legislator and politician on the stage of reality . . . the House of Representatives.

When former Senator George Murphy came to the Senate in the mid-sixties, he would often typecast his Senate colleagues in a speech. A veteran actor, still seen on the late, late television shows, the Republican from California said Democratic Senators Robert and Edward Kennedy would not play the leads in any movie he was directing. He said the Kennedys did not look like senators. They didn't even look like the polo players they've been purported to resemble. The Hollywood actor turned senator said the Kennedys were Wall Street stockbrokers right up to the cut of their chins, and their voice levels.

RMER SENATOR GEORGE MURPHY (left) OF CALIFORNIA TO FORMER SENATOR ORTON OF KENTUCKY: Let's ham it up with Mark Twain's Jumping Frog of laveras County.

Humphrey an Emmett Kelly Clown

For clowns in the Emmett Kelly tradition, Senator Murphy would be torn between offering the part to Senator Hubert Humphrey of Minnesota or Senator Russell Long of Louisiana. Without an ounce of makeup, he said Republican Senator Jacob Javits of New York was a perfect lawyer for the good guys. And if there was a part for an actor in the script, Senator Murphy said he would have given it to the late Senate Minority Leader Everett Dirksen of Illinois.

In his projected movie Senator Murphy would offer the starring role of senator to his colleague Senator Stuart Symington of Missouri, a Democrat. For supporting senator roles, he would use Republican Senator Peter Dominick of Colorado, and two senators who have since left the upper house—Florida Senator Spessard Holland of Florida, and Ohio Senator Frank Lausche.

The former Hollywood movie star also added humor to his speeches by casting a Western from the Senate and then executive branch of the government. For the best male John Wayne type hero, he suggested President Lyndon B. Johnson. Senator Russell B. Long of Louisiana was a natural "Bonanza" lead, with a Louisiana drawl. Murphy also said he would cast Republican Senator John Tower of Texas as a Pat Boone character, saturated with sincerity, personal responsibility, and patriotism. Former Senator Ralph Yarborough of Texas, he saw as a type who would always be at the head of the posse.

And what about heavies or villains and their protagonists?

Senator Murphy said he would ask his Democratic colleague Sam Ervin of North Carolina to be the judge, whether he wanted him to wind up with the good or the bad guys. Former Democratic Senator Pat McNamara of Michigan he would ask to play either the honest or the crooked banker. Former Democratic Senator Mike Monroney of Oklahoma he said looked more like a sheriff than anybody available in the movie capital at the time.

Campaigning Is Taking the Show on the Road

After one speech type-casting his colleagues, somebody asked Murphy why he suggested mostly Democrats for his projected movie?

The Senator looked surprised. Then he commented, "Well, that is interesting. I did, didn't I?"

Veteran actor George Murphy also noted similarities between the performance of a member of Congress and an actor. He said theatre is not only a building where professional actors act out their plays. It is any place where events take place. That makes all the world a stage, and in a particular way the Senate and House chambers.

To be effective, every person trying for elective office today must have some histrionic talent, Murphy said. This is especially true when men strive for national office. Timing and pacing are as essential to good speaking in the home district, on the Senate and House floors, or on public affairs and talk shows on television and radio, as they are in the movies and on the legitimate stage. And when a member of Congress indulges in the politics of humor, the necessity for histrionic talent is compounded.

Murphy sees campaigning as a lot like taking a show on the road. As does a good actor, a politician must know how to express ideas and thoughts intelligently and concisely. He should be able to speak and think effectively on his feet in the same way as does a good theatrical performer. Also, out campaigning the politician must rest when he can as does the actor. A tired candidate or performer is worse than no candidate or no performer. And again when the politician indulges in the politics of humor, the urgency of all these things so essential to the actor's success is compounded.

A HAPPENING IS A HAPPENING IS A HAPPENING

Another member of Congress said he saw similarities between the political arena and the theatre of mixed means.

He noted that in this new form of theatre, components like language, music and technology function nonsynchronously in happenings. He said to politicians performing on the stage of reality, this is nothing new. The man running for elective office has always been communicating in a theatre of mixed means, replete with happenings. For him modern technology has only added a few dimensions.

In a campaigning situation at the turn of the century, a political happening might simply have meant the candidate's turning up with a band on the courthouse steps to speak and offer a little Sousa music. The crowd that shows, turns out to be ten people, two in baby buggies. In that era the candidate could use the politics of humor by saying a few amusing words to eight of the people in the crowd, kiss the two in the baby buggies, and make tracks to greener political pastures.

Mixed Drinks and Mixed Means

A somewhat similar happening today would be complicated by the television cameras. When the crowd fills only the first two rows of a union hall where the candidate is to speak, it could be politically disastrous with the television cameras taking pictures of the empty seats. Nor can the candidate say something funny, kiss a few babies, and move on as in other days. He has to put that mini-crowd into a smaller place where the scarcity isn't carried from coast to coast on television.

This member of Congress asked that his comments comparing happenings in politics and in the theatre of mixed means, be kept anonymous. He said it might seem far out political caution, but somebody reading the book might confuse mixed means with mixed drinks. He had a close race coming up in his area. Besides he wasn't sure that constituents liked to think that their congressman was acting or playing a part. It sounded as if their representative was phoney.

Republican Representative John H. Rousselot of California on the other hand admits frankly that the business of a member of Congress is to communicate above all things. An articulate man with the talents and speaking abilities and grace of an actor finds it much easier to communicate than someone not so blessed.

And still in the histrionic groove, certain members of Congress are more affected by a sympathetic and responsive audience than others.

A few years back reporters in the press gallery could always tell how long former Democratic Senator Wayne Morse of Oregon would talk on the floor of the Senate chamber, by looking over at the Senate family gallery. If Mrs. Morse was there, he would go on for half an hour. If she had a constituent or two with her, it would be closer to an hour. However, if there was nobody up there listening to him, and only a few yawning colleagues on the Senate floor, Morse could wrap up whatever he had to say in five minutes flat.

On the other hand, Senator William Fulbright's apparent lack of interest in, or complete indifference to, the size or shape of his audience in the Senate chamber or hearing room, can give a beginning reporter a real bum steer about the significance or importance of what he has to say. His voice is often low, mildly querulous, and laden with a seeming bored indifference, while he makes some of the wisest and wittiest pronouncements on Capitol Hill.

CONGRESSIONAL GHOST WRITER: If the boss hits the bottle or snarls at the help, may be the speech I just gave him.
Dev O'Neill Pho

CHAPTER EIGHTEEN

Ghost-to-Ghost Hookup

CRYSTAL CITY OF THE GHOST WRITER

And obliquely but importantly related to the subject of the politician as actor is the question: Does the Congressman have a script for his funny lines? How many are his, and how many are somebody else's? When he delivers a funny speech, did he write it himself, or was someone else responsible for it? And is the humorous material original, or is it a matter of simply pinching a few gags from Old Joe's Jokebook, a paid-for joke service, and *Mad* Magazine. Or does somebody do a rewrite on some yarn from Paul Bunyan or Finley Peter Dunne, and effectively interlard the purloined humor between statistics and fact?

The answers are as varied as each of the 535 members of Congress. For it should be made perfectly clear that some congressmen do have their speeches written. Some do not.

Also some admit it, and some do not.

A brief look at the relations between members of Congress and their ghost writers should offer a beginning understanding of the personality, talent, and team play complications involved in dishing congressional humor.

To begin with, the nation's capital is the crystal city of the ghost writer who does any kind of speeches.

And, of course, the Congress is the crystal city within that crystal city.

Nearly all speech writers begin by being idealistic, scholarly, and sensitive.

Shades of Fred Allen's Senator Claghorn

When they first come to work on Capitol Hill, they aspire to be Alexander Hamiltons penning oratory for George Washington. And they suffer an initial shock, when they find themselves prostituting their prose for a member of Congress, who by the nature of living politics, takes on an occasional shade of the Senator Claghorn of radio comedian Fred Allen's famed "Allen's Alley."

In the beginning, they also feel depressed when their congressman doesn't deliver a speech they have written. Then at some time they begin to dig the ghosting groove. They become increasingly cynical, and finally evidence their mature professionalism, when they are glad the boss doesn't deliver a speech. With a little updating it can be rewritten in the future, and the saved time used for coffee breaks in the Senate and House restaurants.

And, of course, when humor is involved, the very personal nature of laughter doubles the intensity of the whole syndrome of emotional and intellectual reactions in the speech writer.

By Any Other Name Would Smell

And now a further explanatory digression in the cause of a clearer understanding of all speech writers connected with the Congress.

If all the ghosts aprowl on Capitol Hill, whether their output is serious or humorous, were identified as such, the place would smell like a graveyard. But they are seldom so labeled. A whole nest of them haunt the Library of Congress, for example, where the faceless ones are brilliant slaves listed as experts and researchers. Their talents and writing skills are available for free to any member of Congress. Then there are the writers right at desks in the offices of the members of Congress, and on the staffs of the congressional committees. They are called researchers, speech writers, specialists, experts, scholars, press officers, clerks, administrative aides . . . you name it, some ghost is so labeled. In an inverted modesty, one woman speech writer even identified herself as a char, when asked what she did on Capitol Hill.

As to their previous background, some are newsmen and newswomen who leave the legitimate news reservation to ghost, when the kids want a swimming pool in McLean, Virginia. Others are the novelists of uncertain age who never made the book, instructors in American government who want to be closer to their subject than a textbook and a lecture platform, young political science majors who hope to one day make the legislature themselves, and aging political science majors who never did.

Big Brain and Dim Wit

A Washington wit wrapped up the ghost-member-of-Congress cooperation as the information in one mind mixing it up with the hot air and histrionics of the other.

In fact all the ghost writer stories on Capitol Hill play on the same theme. The ghost is a big brain and a bigger wit. The member of Congress is a small brain and a dim wit. And when the ghost writer also gives the congressman the humor in his speeches, in the ghostly jokes that rattle their bones around Capitol Hill, he becomes an even bigger wit for a dimmer witted boss. This is because the poltergeists or their legitimate press colleagues make up most of the jokes. One contribution to this fiction is about the Senator waiting for his host to finish the speech so he would know what he was going to say. Another is about the solon watching his distinguished colleagues give a snide television talk, and shouting, "I'm not going to let his speech writer say that about my speech writer."

Still another concerns the ghost writer who got fired. The Senator told him frankly his speeches smelled.

He answered, "I label myself dead and smell legitimately. You also smell, Senator, but illegitimately and prematurely. Some of your deluded constituents think you're still alive."

Now most members of Congress get along well with their ghost writers if they have one. Sometimes they even like the individual who writes their speeches, which is of course, because members of Congress are usually cautious in selecting their personal ghosts. The speech writer must be a kind of alter-ego for the congressman—know not only what he thinks about legislation, but what he doesn't think and should think. And also many congressmen believe that a perceptive hep speech writer shouldn't need more than three minutes with his boss to get what the congressman wants to say, and should produce on *Congressional Record* deadline.

Hits the Bottle or Snarls at the Help

In fact, if a member of Congress hits the bottle or snarls at the help, it may not be his wife or the opposition. His ghost might not quite understand him, or might have gotten mad and gone literary, or snydicated himself under a byline. A member of Congress soon finds he does well if he selects a ghost who is sufficiently mediocre, so as not to be tempted to desert the legislator for screen or television writing, or public relations in the private sector, or to go back to the legitimate press. And of course, when the ghost gives his boss the dividend of humor for his GS 14 salary, all these potentials for him wanting out are intensified.

And the experienced speech writer is equally selective about the member of Congress he ghosts. He likes one he doesn't have to wait outside committee rooms to see, when he needs to know his boss's pitch on the inclusion of liver transplant operations in an amendment to the medicare bill, the amount of sewerage Lake Michigan can take, or what sanitized landfills can do for the nation's trash troubles. Also the writer likes to know before he takes the job, exactly what his congressman wants for the $15,000 a year he is paying.

Some members of Congress ask their ghosts to produce a whole speech—bones, flesh, bombast, and cliches—wrapped in a neat typing job. These, by the way, are the fellows who usually won't admit to having a ghost.

Others ask for only a skeleton outline.

Still others prefer the flesh of fact and research.

PROTECTION AGAINST PRESS MANGLING

It should also be pointed out that members of Congress use different methods of getting their speeches to the podium on time.

The late Representative James Fulton of Pennsylvania had the aides in his office prepare tons of research with the help of the ghosts at the Library of Congress. He stirred his own ideas into this thick potage, dictated it, and always turned up with a palatable brew.

Except for rare heavily-researched speeches, by reason of their subject matter, Representative William B. Widnall (R-N.J.), for example, prefers to speak extemporaneously. He likes to see his own ideas in note form on a half sheet of paper, enriched here and there by ideas tossed him by staff members. But he uses his staff as what might be called demi-ghosts, to get the stuff down on paper as a protection against mangling by the press. He feels a speech in the hand is worth three in the mouth, if a congressman is misquoted and needs a retraction.

The former Senator Ralph Yarborough (D-Tex.) always liked good basic research from his staff. He also liked to get together with them, and toss around ideas relevant to the subject of the speech. These he altered, revised, changed, edited, rewrote, and finally got a finished product down on paper. But this big man from the Lone Star State felt a speech must match an audience, and he could only tell that when he saw the audience. As a result, most of the time the written speech was never given. The ghost's choice anecdote or joke salvaged even in the Senator's rewrites, was never voiced by his boss.

And, of course, some members of Congress buck the ghost system. They write their own speeches, which forces their hired ghost to take constituents to lunch, answer mail, and talk with lobbyists. A case in point is James Southerland. For three years he wrote speeches for former Secretary of Commerce Luther Hodges and, on the strength of his top flight performance, was hired as administrative aide to Representative Claude Pepper. On the job he discovered his new boss visualizes his speeches paragraph by paragraph in his own mind, and doesn't need a speech writer. And as far as a gag or anecdote is concerned, the Congressman from Florida has his own bag of tricks there, too.

The Oratorically Underprivileged

A speech writer on the staff of former Senator George Murphy had equally little to do. The one-time actor and labor leader wrote his own speeches, except for an occasional idea a staffer threw him on the way in or out. Or rather, the Senator spoke his own, for he used only a few notes.

This is all fine when the congressman has the experience and skill of the Democratic representative from Florida and the former Republican Senator from California. But when a legislator is educationally as well as oratorically underprivileged, the result can be dismal. Besides, nobody believes the congressman writes his speeches anyway. It is simply rumored around he is haunted by a lousy ghost.

And to return briefly to the categorizing of speech writers, the best nonresident Capitol Hill ghost, of course, is the lobby ghost. He is highly paid to know oil, gas, or sesame seeds. A request for information about this subject is so well put together it requires little to turn it into brilliant oratorical shape for a speech. Providing the member of Congress is well aware of his source, and the interests of that source, the lobby ghost should not be discounted when the congressman needs an expert on the subject, trimmed up happily with some embroidery of humor. A lobby ghost has as part of his working equipment a card catalogue of every joke and anecdote that's ever been concocted in the area of his specialite— whether it be oil, gas, or sesame seeds.

And there are also some interesting types who do not fall simply into the general Capitol Hill ectoplasmic pattern of naive and cynical ghosts. There is the occasional fellow who passionately wants to save some vanishing animal or bird species, or get funds for day care centers

. . . through the congressman's speeches. Another Svengali fellow gloats on the powers he exerts when he fills what he calls the semi-vacuum of the congressman's mind.

Nosing Out Ghost Dropouts

And, of course, because it is what this book is all about, there is also the would-be humorist who could never make the commercial magazine market on his own byline. This one relishes hearing his well-baked or half-baked wit rendered in the congressman's dulcet tones, and grabbed by a newspaper columnist in the press gallery.

More senators than representatives employ full time ghost writers. They have larger budgets for this kind of embellishment. One congressman suggested that most of his confreres, including himself, would have liked to have a good ghost haunting their premises. It's just that they couldn't afford them. He said this might be remedied by the federal government organizing some sort of ghost corps. You know, nosing out ghost dropouts, and paying for their rehabilitation while they work in a congressman's office. He said he would have given any three ghost dropouts plenty of speeches to write for him . . . if he could have gotten funds to pay them from such a Ghost Corps.

FROM THE OLD BOY'S JOLLY HEART

Now a congressman usually believes if he steals facts, platitudes, cliches, and statistics for a speech, he steals trash. His help also believes this. However, to even intimate he pinches humor from Archie Bunker or pays for it from his ghost writer, is to question his good name. There's something intimate and personal about humor, something a shade shady about accepting laughs from anybody else. Others consider humor belongs to everyone, and the best things in life are freebies. They pinch a pun from "Laugh-In," a bit of gallows humor from a ghost, or a bromide from their teenage kid, and deliver it in speech without any thought about who started the whole funny ball rolling anyway. Many speech writers, once they know where the congressman stands on any subject, outline or write serious speeches for him. A much smaller number also supply him with the humor that garnishes the facts. Most of the laughs the congressman dishes are his own, off-the-cuff, extemporaneous, right from the jolly heart of the dear old boy . . . as original as anything he's ever thought of himself, heard, or picked up from anybody anywhere.

A couple of congressmen have admitted off the record that their ghosts or researchers sometimes did offer them humor, but they didn't use it. It wasn't very good.

Some congressmen buy a joke service which makes the writing lives of their speech writers easier when the boss wants humor supplied. The puns and political sallies with which the boss tops and concludes his speeches may then be picked up from pages which come regularly to the office.

The ghost writer for one customer of the joke service put it this way:

"My congressman is only an hour by car from Washington to his district. He simply cannot refuse a speaking engagement. Without that joke service he'd have to hire Bob Hope away from his gag writers to get enough funny stories to begin all the speeches he has to make."

Zsa Zsa Gabor's Fifth Husband

One freshmen member of Congress, however, just may have bought and swallowed that or some other fun source too soon, or his speech writer was a naive type as yet unaware of the bromides of Capitol Hill. Selected by the Washington Press Club by lot as one of its congressional dinner speakers, Representative William S. Cohen (R-Me.) said he felt in his new legislative role "like Zsa Zsa Gabor's fifth husband . . . I know how to do it, but I'm not so sure I can make it interesting." At least a half dozen members of Congress had used this analogy in various contexts during the past year. Two of greater vintage offered it with a variation on the theme. They felt like Barbara Hutton's seventh husband.

And at least six have also used this one in the past year to assure their audiences they are really modest, humble types because their wives have made them so:

When I come to a function like the one I am attending where everybody says such glowing things about me in an introduction, I get to believing them. Once not so long ago, when I was coming from just such a laudatory gathering, I asked my wife, "I wonder how many important people there are in the world?" To which my wife replied, "One less than you think there is, dear."

The general opinion also seems to be that members of Congress who want humor in their speeches are particularly hazardous fellows to ghost. This is because their reaction when their ghost written speech is received with loud laughter by an audience, varies with the size and quality of the vanity of the member of Congress.

One long time jaded speech writer on Capitol Hill says his present congressman inclines to give him a Christmas or other-day-of-the-year bonus when he does a really funny speech. However, a previous boss wouldn't speak to him for three weeks, after he wrote a talk for him that was marvelously funny, and brought down an auditorium somewhere or other. That congressman wanted to bask alone in the glow that lingers in the wake of the successful humorist. It embarrassed him to think that he didn't write the speech. Still another former boss of this speech writer would never permit the ghost to be in the audience. The congressman simply fluffed his lines when he knew his speech writer was among the people listening to him.

Another speech writer who got fed up with his congressman boss decided to quit. But before he went, he wanted to dish one little nasty to the member of Congress who had been making his writing life miserable for a succession of years. He gave his boss a ten-page speech interlarded with amusing anecdotes pertinent to the legislation he was discussing. On page seven in the middle of a really great yarn he stopped and wrote, "FROM HERE ON, YOU ARE ON YOUR OWN, YOU SON OF A BITCH."

KENNEDY GHOST IN THE WHITE HOUSE?

About one year after President Richard Nixon won the election to his first term in the White House, Democratic Representative Neal Smith of Iowa had some words to say on the floor of the House of Representatives about the chief executive's consumer message to the legislative body.

Mr. Speaker, President Nixon was inaugurated on January 20. In the months that followed, one of the questions of great interest was what would be his policy on consumer legislation. For ten months and ten days there was almost stone silence at the White House except to say that they needed more time to formulate a great important announcement.

Finally on October 30, the Doorkeeper of the House, Fishbait Miller, appeared in the center aisle and said:

"Mr. Speaker—a message from the President of the United States."

It had arrived. The long-awaited message directed to consumers. It proclaimed that consumers shall have a bill of rights and was couched in such language as to indicate that it was an original document to be laid beside the Declaration of Independence and the Magna Carta and remembered for all time; but Mr. Speaker, I now find that this great document, which took ten months and ten days to prepare, was really a copy of one page from the consumer message John F. Kennedy sent to Congress seven and a half years before—on March 15, 1962.

The message lists the same four rights and is so much the same that the same speech writer has somehow managed to stay at the White House under this new administration. Since it took him ten months and ten days to find this document that was written seven and a half years ago, he must be in such an obscure corner that nobody notices whether he is working.

Save the Congress a Lot of Time

If it takes ten months and ten days to copy a former President's message, and this is to be the pattern of other messages we have been waiting on for so long, I suggest that it might save the Congress a lot of time, in lieu of a whole string of such messages that are now likely to come, if the President would just send up a one-page request for permission to insert in the Congressional Record all the messages delivered by Presidents Kennedy and Johnson as if delivered by him. If he were to do that, he could reduce the rising cost of White House staff, help to balance the budget, or at least afford more time which is obviously needed for the White House speech writers to research material for Agnew's speeches.

*   *   *

And in the event anybody isn't aware that there are ghostwriting gems the equivalent of film reel jewels on the cutting room floor . . . there are. Sometimes a ghost writes a really good, funny speech for his congressman—one worthy of Art Buchwald space in the nation's newspapers—and the congressman drops it in the wastepaper basket. This one, for example, was purportedly prepared for delivery at a banquet of shoe manufacturers in the Midwest. It was apparently given the old drop into the basket. The legislator said it was because he wasn't sure the shoe manufacturers would get all the subtleties. The ghost says it was because the congressman himself liked to go barefooted—around the house, of course, not the office. The ghost writer called the speech, "If Ever I Should Shoe You."

TO SHOE OR NOT TO SHOE THE HUMAN FOOT

Ladies and Gentlemen of the Shoe Business:

I know you people are worried about the new barefoot fad that's sweeping the country.

But I want to assure you of something.

The world might be in a mess, but it's not about to walk out of the mess barefooted. It's going to walk out of it shoed and booted.

It is true that right now to bare or not to bare the human foot is stirring up a lot of controversy. As many shades of opinion swirl around the question, as around whether or not baby orchids should float in the champagne, or meat of the fowl should intrude on the hot dog.

Let me describe some of these shades of opinion.

One area around which the barefoot controversy swirls is freedom. The young go barefoot in the park, on the city's concrete streets, lawns with pesticides, anywhere. They vote with their naked feet for freedom from fathers, the Tricia Nixon image, the consumer society, fluoride toothpaste, clean sheeted beds, anything. The over-thirties may go micromini or Bearded Apostle, but barefoot in the street they will not go. They sneer in their shoes, making snide noises about hookworm, pinworm, broken glass on the streets.

The foot doctors themselves agree only on clean white sand, where any bare foot may walk safely whether on the beach or in the kindergarten playbox. Beyond the sand, one doctor contends—unless the skin is broken—the bare foot is healthier walking or running anywhere, than if it were shoed. Another wouldn't put his own foot down on his bedroom floor without a slipper under its sole. A cynical type insists if the warts don't get you, the bunions will, so enjoy your feet, they're safer than you think. Another reminds there's the broken glass thing—barefoot in the park, but not in the dark. Another was blunt. He offered one sentence between a warted foot and one that was flat . . . great for business. A voice on the American Podiatrists Association telephone was nervous and noncommittal on bare feet. No pamphlets, no brochures, no books, no official position on the subject excepting an implied admission that people are not born with shoes on.

As a matter of fact some podiatrists, by placing their address and profession prominently on a tree trunk poster during rock festivals, have managed to hang about for business in the same fashion as certain lawyer types chase ambulances.

Never Could I Shoe You at All

And it should be pointed out that season is not involved in the bare foot cult. With parody apologies to Camelot, this is clearly illustrated in the ode of the young to their feet, sung by flower children at a shu-out:

"If ever I should shoe you, it wouldn't be in summer,

Seeing you in summer, your arch streaked with sunlight, your heel red as flame,

Your toes with a luster that puts jewels to shame.
How could I shoe you in autumn?
I have seen how you sparkle when fall nips the air.
And could I ever boot you, running frostily thru the snow?
Or on a wintry evening, when you catch the fire's glow?
If ever I could shoe you, how could it be in springtime?
Knowing how in springtime, I am bewitched by you so?
Oh no, not in springtime, summer, winter or fall!
No, never could I shoe you at all."

Then there is the controversy as to whether the bare foot is something that induces romantic thoughts. Some contend the Renoir pink foot can indeed be on the sexy side, can have more erotic voltage than a Midsummer Night's Dream potion, especially on an effective rug, on early morning lawns, or strips of sand. Then there are others who class the bare foot, particularly unwashed, belonging to anybody to be part of the make-up kit of the world's uglies—the toad, Cinderella's stepsisters, and the Hansel and Gretel witch. In fact when it's been around on the city's sidewalks, some hold the bare foot inspires a decidedly unromantic reaction, excepting in a Samuel Beckett or Henry Miller character.

But let me offer you shoe manufacturers a word to the foot sartorialwise. Do you know what will get the shoes back on the barefooted, and restore to you this substantial part of your market? It will be the same thing the girl Penguin found out in Anatole France's Penguin Island. Anything anybody's got that isn't the greatest, looks better under chiffon or velvet or something. That goes for feet too. . . .

The last page or two got lost somewhere between the Congressman's desk and the wastepaper basket from which it was recovered. And before the Congress had adjourned, the speech writer was back in the underpaid writing press, and his editor was asking the aspiring humorist to stick to straight news. If he wanted to write funny, he should do it on his own time.

*　　*　　*

And inversely, a cool-headed speech writer sometimes keeps his congressman out of a lot of trouble. After the visit of President Richard Nixon to China, a congressman with a legislative imagination that sometimes runs amuck, returned to his office after a six to eight reception at a place where there was a plethora of Chinoiserie in the decor. He sat down at his typewriter and wrote this draft of a campaign speech he intended to give at a Sunday political rally in his own home district over the weekend. He left it on his ghost's typewriter to read.

PUT DOWN IN THE WORK POT

Ladies and Gentlemen:

In this Congress I intend to introduce legislation that will use some of the best of the discipline of Mao's China.

It will require all citizens of the United States, whether intellectuals or executives or writers or artists or white collar types to work in the soil, or in other grubby, nitty-gritty jobs, several months of each year.

There are a lot of us in this country who would like to see Spiro Agnew and Henry Kissinger and David Eisenhower picking tomatoes in some United States equivalent of the Imperial Valley. I personally am fascinated, hypnotized by the image of Spiro down on his stiff knees for two whole months every year, mean and unhumbled. And I'm sure a lot of other citizens of the United States feel the same way. Think of Kissinger, with his fat hands in the dirt for the same sixty consecutive days, trying to see through his thick glasses, to put a rice plant or a cotton plant or some other plant into some reluctant soil. The boyish grin of David Eisenhower dissolving fast in the muddy muck of valeting for farm animals.

All the people who have been doing the nation's dirty, dangerous, dull, and stupid jobs would be behind anybody who would introduce legislation that would put their bosses in their same mucky situation two months of every year. To say nothing of channeling a few types they know and don't like in the same situation, and some more they don't know, but can't stand anyway.

The Muck and Gluck of A House

Then there are all the types who have been forced by the patterns of snobbery into teaching, office routines, and clergy, medicine, the law . . . when all they really liked to do was work with their hands and their backs on farms, a work bench, in a stable, on a construction gang, and cleaning up the muck and gluck of a house.

Politicians on the whole do not suffer from this kind of Puritan work worship affliction. But I am personally astute enough to know some people do. I am also aware that all the do-it-yourself weekending had never satisfied the yearning for this kind of thing on the part of certain types who would indeed welcome that promise of dirty work in their pot.

And then, of course, there is a whole potpourri of folks who never know what to do with their vacations anyway, types who can't stand family vacations. Also there are the harnessed who can't get comfortably out of a harness for a few weeks or months, the masochists who get a real satisfaction out of having to do by law something they do not like to do.

The idea of being forced by law to go anywhere and work in the soil and in other grubby jobs would for them not be something to be frowned upon, to hate, to vote against. Instead it would be something to be glad about, to prefer, to vote for.

Not that I don't know that I will have strong opposition. The other camp is a big one. Roughly half the population are in it!

All the chronically and inherently lazy who have established themselves at a desk, a stool in a lab, on faculty, and government seats, will be against it. So will all those who have made a pile one way or another, or their grandfather has. Two months of dirty work will be the last thing these types want in their work pots.

But even these may shift to my way of thinking, for while they may have to put in their lick of work, they will know that all the people they can't stand will be shucking corn, row on row in some already frostbitten cornfield, their hands ungloved and blue with cold. That is, if corn is shucked after a frost. I haven't the foggiest really.

Think of how so many of the people in today's Republic of China must have enjoyed seeing all those types symbolized in the figures on teacups and vases, put down in the work pot. Like our beatniks, hippies, flower children, they did nothing except loll about in kimonos and coolie hats near ponds and gazebos pagodas, and wherever they can find a gnarled tree or bamboo and sip tea and rice wine and fish . . . for fish they never catch . . . or never clean. Think of what it must have meant to the people of China to see these types cleaning fish day after day . . . gutsy fish with hard to cut-off heads and full of scales. And also see them work seven days a week, ten hours a day surrounded and permeated with the smell of fish. . . .

When the congressman came in the following day, he found a note on the speech from his ghost:

"This is simply bananas politically! You must have gone ape to think you could pull anything like this."

In the cool of the working morning, minus the glow of the Scotch imbibed at the reception and removed from the Chinoiserie decor, the congressman agreed. He was re-elected.

SENATOR ROBERT TAFT (left): We must act decisively to improve the quality of life in our cities .

Republican Policy Committee Photo

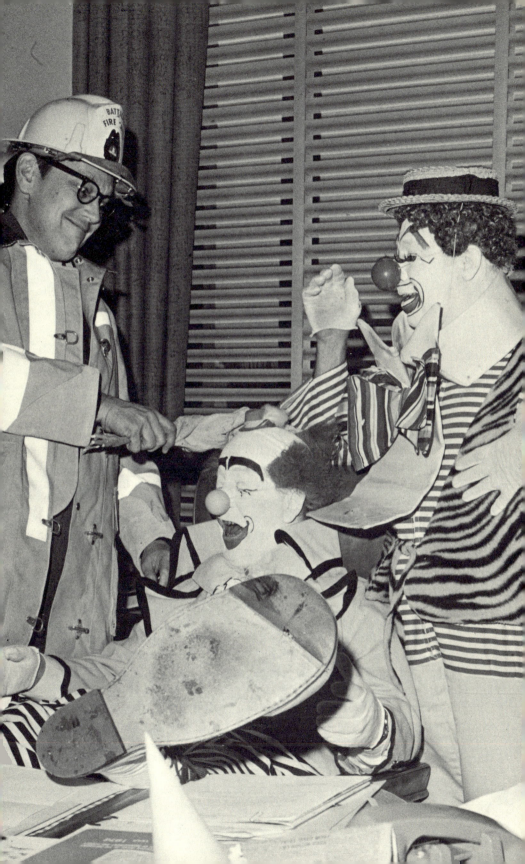

CHAPTER NINETEEN

Some Congressmen Are Funny and Some Are Not

REAL ALICE, ASKING IF THE BOSS IS FUNNY

So much of the humor on Capitol Hill is a fleeting and nebulous thing. It is gone with the hot air of the moment.

And some of this unconscious laughter turned up in the process of gathering the material for this book.

It came mostly in sidebar telephone brushes with the aides of a senator or representative. When asked for some of the congressman's humorous speeches or exchanges on the floor, one feminine voice from the office of a southern member was indignant:

"Ma'am," she said, "Do you think my congressman is in Washington having a ball! My boss is a serious man. He isn't about to strut around being funny like some others I know."

Another said her boss was an absolute riot—always cutting up in the office and when he gave speeches. But none of it ever got written down so it sounded right. It was gone almost as soon as he said it. She knew, because she once tried to write some of it down. And it was peculiar. It didn't come out real funny at all . . . written down, that is. She couldn't dig why.

Then a voice—blunt, masculine, sepulchral—that seemed to emanate from the Capitol Dome itself—began by asking that he be identified only as an unusually reliable source. Then he added, "That's real Alice, asking if the boss is funny. He is, darling, but he doesn't know it . . . hasn't the foggiest. And I'm not about to tell him. I couldn't get twenty thousand anywhere else . . . not anywhere."

Still another voice, that also asked not to be identified, confided his boss was the dullest guy in the decadent East and points west. Not, of course, that he wasn't a superb legislator.

A third voice—also a man's—said his congressman wasn't about to mix it up in anything dirty like this project. The proposition was then made clearer on the telephone. All that was wanted was a laugh from the congressman—and that in writing. The book wasn't about to include outhouse humor in the graffiti or Rabelaisian grooves. An interview with the congressman wasn't at all necessary. The aide was not convinced and still considered the proposed book something for the city's starlings.

During the next hour of telephoning, the quest for laughs took on shades of editorial prostitution, or at least had an aura of a political demi-monde.

KEATING'S DUMB CLUCK STUFF

Another press secretary nastily named names.

She said her congressman was a dignified type who wasn't always dishing corny dumb cluck stuff like the former Senator Kenneth Keating (R-N.Y.). However, once she said that she then admitted her congressman did occasionally use a little anecdote. But his occasional indulgence was in something of rare and original excellence . . . real gems in comparison with the shoddy, flashy costume jewelry stuff dished by Senator Keating. A sensation was experienced by the author of being promised a filched goodie under the counter, without paying for it in proper legitimate coinage. The goodie was never received.

The administrative aide of a member of the House Appropriations Committee who had been on Capitol Hill for twenty years was equally hung up. He said his congressman found nothing to be funny about, with everybody saying gimme-gimme. Encouraged, he also digressed to his own personal gripes. He said with all the unsolved problems, his congressman slaved all the time. So did his staff. That was why most members of Congress didn't live long enough to enjoy the benefits of the House retirement plan . . . only their widows.

Federal Government Is No Baby Sitter

He digressed to say everything was getting to be much too big. The population was growing, programs were proliferating, and more taxes were being collected. His congressman had nearly doubled his constituency in redistricting, and they all expected the Federal government to be a baby sitter and a substitute for the family. And just as he was making noises threatening to hang up, he said the country wouldn't lose anything if every college in the country was closed. The universities were unnecessary middlemen for knowledge. Young people should be chucked into libraries, and should sink or swim on their ability to sit and absorb knowledge from books.

UDALL NOT PREGNANT WITH BOOK

A man on the staff of a member of the House who is considered to be one of the funniest men in the House of Representatives—Representative Morris K. Udall (D-Ariz.)—explained immediately that the congressman had himself been for the past twenty-five years composing and collecting fat files of humor. On the other end of the telephone it was as promptly admitted that Udall was hardly a member of the Congress who would want to contribute to a book on congressional humor. He apparently had enough research and original stuff to do a couple volumes on the same subject himself. But would he please not bring it out before this book. However, the author's social antenna was bent by that time and not getting through, for the staff member quickly protested. The congressman was by no means about to have a book. He didn't even have a faint literary gleam in his eye. If Representative Udall published the best of what he had in a volume which anybody could buy for a few bucks, everybody would have all the wonderful stories he had so painstakingly collected in his fat files. He wasn't about to dish any laugh handouts to anybody.

Also the months planned for the researching, editing, and writing of this book—August to February—posed certain advantages and disadvantages in the collecting of the humorous material.

Defeated or retiring members of Congress and their staffs, for example, either over-reacted or under-reacted. Some were anxious to salvage their own or the congressman's laughs for posterity. They sent material by messenger that wasn't funny at all, or some wispy offerings in the category of sick jokes, bromides, or pale puns. Others were much too busy to dig up the laughing past of their on-his-way-out boss. They were busy playing the rat leaving the sinking legislative ship, looking for another job, or rushing to catch a plane for the Christmas holidays. Two suggested a deal. If in the telephoning, vacancies were heard about on the staffs of other congressmen, could they be alerted. And if once tipped off, they got the job, they would go through for laughs, every file of both the defeated or retiring congressman and those of their new boss as well.

WHEN THE SPRING SETS IN WITH DAFFODILS

Also some voices from the congressional offices, when asked for a few of the congressman's laughs preserved in typewritten, mimeographed, or Xeroxed prose, turned out to be professional buck passers of rare skill. Their voices, always warm with the hope of humor on the way, suggested a call back after the election, after the Christmas holidays, after Congress reconvened in early January, or when the spring set in with daffodils and azaleas on Capitol Hill.

And in that order, of course.

Or their voices, saturated with the futility of it all, suggested the congressman handled that sort of thing himself. But try to find the congressman in the last months of an election year! Before the first Tuesday in November, he is campaigning or mending fences. After that, planning his upcoming hearings, drafting bills or junketing—paying his wife's expenses, of course. Or his stuff is packed in boxes ready to send to the State University Library . . . if they want it, that is. Or he is looking around for a Washington job that needs his services at a salary of five figures.

On one late call, the congressman came to the telephone himself. He said he would send some stuff over, if it would be labeled homespun philosophy and not humor. The stuff came. It was neither homespun philosophy nor humor . . . not by any stretch of opportunist labeling.

Another member of the House came to the telephone and said he never found anything funny anywhere . . . what with the "Veetnam" War and libbing women. Besides he lost and had thrown everything out. He added he was an ecology buff, even where he himself was concerned. He didn't think even a member's funny hot air should be preserved beyond his term of office . . . what with all the air pollution.

Democratic Representative Andy Jacobs of Indiana, who had just been defeated and was everybody in his own office, talked for an hour.

A FUNNIER ONE DOWN THE HALL

On one very late call, after the staff man delegated to answer this kind of question had been reputed to be out for lunch, coffee breaking, or busy on three heavy long distance calls thick with crises, a weary char answered the phone.

Asked, "Is the Congressman a funny type?" she answered, "Which one? I do for all of them in the offices on this corridor."

"The one where you are right now?"

"Oh, him. He's not really funny looking, ma'am. But he does wear his hair kind of hippie long . . . what he has of it which looks right obscene on an old man, especially when he's tired from working late. But there's a much funnier looking one down the hall. He has a waxed mustache. They say he's so funny on the floor of the House, when the other members know he's going to speak, they come out of the Men's and everywhere to be on the floor to hear him."

We really have a good thing going at the water gate
Nick Pergola Photo

CHAPTER TWENTY

Congressional Laughter at the Watergate

WATERGATE NO PUBLIC WORKS PROJECT

A tide of savage political laughter has been moving over Capitol Hill in the wake of the Watergate scandal. Some of it is original, some picked off as it wings over, and some is drafted by ghost writers and molded to suit the congressman's laugh style.

Trickles of it began spilling out more than a year ago.

In mid-1972, Republican Senator Robert Dole of Kansas, former Chairman of the Republican National Committee, was telling members of the press that people outside of Washington thought the Watergate was a public works project. Opposition congressmen countered by quoting Lawrence O'Brien, then Chairman of the Democratic National Committee, as saying that the only things the men who broke into their Watergate headquarters would have found were unpaid telephone bills. A mean partisan Republican type was saying the Democratic party headquarters needed fumigating, not bugging.

PLATOON OF POMPOUS PINHEADS

Even before that, in February 1971, in a statement which he called "Foxes in the Chicken Coop," Iowa's Republican Representative Bill Scherle was giving a preview of Watergate. With head rhymes, mixed metaphor, and irony, he was describing the arrogance of the White House inner circle:

Presently promenading piously through the plush paneled offices of the White House is a platoon of pompous pinheads. These incredibly incompetent White House staffers have managed in two short years to embarrass the President in almost every facet of his Chief Executive's post. So skilled have they been in their goof-ups, that the only remaining question is whether they have acted deliberately in their exhibition of stupidity, or have managed to grope their way down the primrose path of pathetic prattling through stark naivete. . . .

*   *   *

Then with the spring of 1973, the flood of congressional comment began. It included everything from shades of irony, to black humor in the mood of Kafka and Beckett, making it perfectly clear that foolishness and not reason often runs the world.

Here are some the congressmen are telling:

One week a White House staffer is on the cover of Time. *The next week he's doing time.*

*   *   *

The Secret Service in the White House used to fight not to go on the Nixon trips. They were on the dull side. Today they're fighting to do the advance on the Leavenworth trip.

*   *   *

In January the White House staffers were fighting to get the lowest license plate numbers. Today they're fighting to see who makes the lowest numbered license plates.

Service bands are playing "Bail for the Chief" instead of "Hail to the Chief."

And that skylab up there. It's heated up because it was weighted down with the lost records relating to the Watergate scandal.

So many people are lining up on the Senate side to tell all they know about the Watergate that the Chairman of the hearings, Senator Sam Ervin, has to say, "Take a number."

*   *   *

Everything goes by the book in the White House. The book is The Godfather. *And when German Chancellor Willy Brandt was here recently what he was really doing was arranging a new German staff for the President.*

Republican William B. Saxbe of Ohio told the press that the attitude of the White House is they don't know what's going on. He adds that maybe it's like that guy playing the piano in a bawdy house, who doesn't know what's going on upstairs. And another midwestern congressman passes it on that White House Press Secretary Ron Ziegler has been saying all previous Nixons are inoperative. Democratic Representative William Ford of Michigan tells his fellow members in the House he is collecting a special fund to pay for television time for Martha Mitchell. Then she may defend her husband, former Attorney General John Mitchell, on prime time.

WATERGATE MUM THE NEW NATIONAL FLOWER

And since the White House aides began to talk, members of Congress are suggesting the President wants indictments with honor. Senator Joseph M. Montoya, Democrat of New Mexico, is saying the White House is cancelling its Sunday Prayer Breakfasts. Operas will be scheduled instead, for Nixon now knows his staffers can sing. In the Democratic cloakroom they are talking about the sign "The Buck Stops Here" which President Nixon put on E. R. Haldeman's desk, and saying a lot of the White House employees are not sleeping too well because Tricky Dick is President.

A southern Democratic congressman is telling another from the same area that the Republican Chief Executive is keeping his campaign promise of removing crime from the streets. He's put it into the White House. The other counters by asking if his colleague has heard about the windows and doors of the White House being reinforced with bars. The police are also turned around with their backs to the street, to watch more carefully the people inside the mansion. And in the Republican cloakroom one member asks another if he heard that the President has declared the Watergate Mum the new national flower, and that the password at the White House is "Pardon."

Democratic Representative Henry B. Gonzalez of Texas says the whole Watergate thing is something Vice President Spiro Agnew cooked up to keep former Democratic Texas Governor John Connally from switching to the GOP. Spiro's not about to be upstaged for the Republican presidential nomination in 1976. And when it was reported that the Vice President was appalled at the handling of the Watergate scandal, he was reminded by congressional wits that the setting sun can also blister. Then when former Governor Connally did switch to the GOP, Representative

Thomas P. O'Neill, Democrat of Massachusetts, was calling it a real first in American history . . . a former Secretary of the Navy getting on a sinking ship.

NIXON ALIVE AND WELL IN THE BUNKER

In the Senate restaurant, they are asking if President Nixon is still alive and well in the White House bunker, and if it's true that they're answering the telephone at the headquarters of CREEP, the Committee for the Re-election of the President, with the statement, "Five to Ten Years." A senator who sometimes thinks in outhouse grooves, is calling former Attorney General Mitchell "Nixon's John," and his former attorney Dean, "Nixon's Other John." And a congressman from a district in spring-flooded east Texas is saying his region is a little wet for this time of year . . . since somebody opened the Water's Gate.

THE KING'S SOUTHERN KRAUTS

One Republican congressman's misanthropic and contrary ghost writer contends—complicated as it is—the Watergate is easier to explain to constituents than the complicated business that goes on between the gleam in a bull's eye and the high price of steak. And a senator's scholarly ghost writer says the Watergate has made one thing perfectly clear—the brand of Mafia that has been resident in the White House. The Executive mansion has always had some kind of Mafia. In the Kennedy Administration it was Irish. In the LBJ Administration it was the Texas Mafia. But in the Nixon Administration, the Mafia outlines were fudged, and that's why it's been hard to figure. Nobody knew whether it was a German or a Southern Rim brand. Some Congressmen were calling the men with predominantly German names, "All the King's Krauts." Others noted most of them had Southern Rim origins. They came from Southern California, through Arizona, and Texas, down to the Florida Keys. Now it's clear it's a Southern Rim German Mafia. A Japanese newsman suggests he should have had a Japanese Mafia. They are not only experts in electronics and bugging, but commit hara-kiri when they fail.

And at the end of the Washington premiere of the "Last Tango in Paris," when Marlon Brando lay dead on the floor, a voice came from the audience saying, "At least it makes us forget the Watergate for a while." And an answering voice said, "Not for long." They were both reported to have been the voices of congressmen.

And, of course, in the wings, former Democratic presidential candidate Senator Eugene McCarthy, Democrat of Minnesota, is saying the difference between politicians and those mixed up in the Watergate scandal is that the former are inclined to accept dry goods like vicuna coats and the latter seem to come and go for money. And he quotes former Senator Paul Douglas, Democrat of Illinois, as saying that no politician should take anything he cannot eat in twenty-four hours.

Then there's Democratic Senator Hubert H. Humphrey of Minnesota saying, "The Watergate is bad public works." And Senator Robert Dole says with bitter irony, "This Mickey Mouse game at Watergate is the kind of game these people play. They revel in cheap stuff, like dropping a leak to the press that you are ousted . . . as for the Republican National Committee we were relegated to the back of the bus . . . no, the truth is that we weren't even on the bus at all."

DOWN AT THE OLDE BULL AND BUSH

Then a Republican Congressman tells a colleague that Allen Drury, author of *Advise and Consent,* is suing the Administration for plagiarism, and the other answers that Truman Capote is writing one about the Watergate called *In Cold Cash.* And Democratic Representative William L. Hungate of Missouri offers a crescendo of the whole Watergate scandal flood of congressional comment by writing the lyrics to a commemorative song in the key of G. It is called "Down by the Old Watergate," and subtitled "Under the Anheuser-Busch" or "Down at the Olde Bull and Bush."

Come, come, and play spy with me,
Down at the old Watergate!
Come, come, come love and lie with me,
Down at the old Watergate!
See the little German band
Ehrlichman und Haldeman,
Don't Martha Mitchell look great!
Come, come, come don't be shy with me,
I'll have the whole FBI with me!
Down at the old Water,
We'll make the police blotter
Down at the old Watergate!

REPRESENTATIVE THOMAS P. O'NEILL (D-Mass.): The Republicans must be out of their tree to think they could get away with that.   Dev O'Neill Photo

This congressional laughter is heard in the Capitol corridors, in the press and visitors' galleries, on the floor of the House of Representatives and of the Senate, and in the restaurants. While melancholy voices are saying the Watergate scandal is a sad and shoddy thing and the mess is threatening the office of the Presidency, the legislative branch is also seeing events as part of the theatre of the political absurd with nothing orderly or logical about them. The Nixon Administration is no longer all prayer breakfasts, cottage cheese with catsup lunches, and neat crew cuts in the Prussian mood. Nixon's private cans of political worms are being opened up, and a cloak and dagger, cops and robbers game it is.

There hasn't been a wave of irony or black humor like this since Senator Thomas Eagleton of Missouri removed himself from the Democratic vice presidential spot and Los Angeles congressmen were saying nobody in Hollywood would hide their visits to a psychiatrist. They bragged about going to a shrink. And Massachusetts congressmen were saying . . . at least when Senator Edward Kennedy was on a couch, it was always with a girl.

*SENATOR EDWARD MOORE KENNEDY: Now there's nothing political in thes
congressional hearings.*

Dev O'Neill Pho

Index